Preface

I didn't do too well at secondary modern, so once I'd left I went to night school. NO, not to sleep, but to learn basic electronics.
Mum and Dad bought me a Philips engineering kit - you know, the ones with springs and components and a holey board on which to arrange them. I loved it; I inadvertently made a transmitter out of a three-transistor radio receiver, just by experimenting, but my Dad wasn't impressed, as it took him quite a while to work out why his radio programmes were disrupted…

I remember working in our electricians' work shed, making microphone stands out of ¾ inch conduit (soon to become 20mm in '71) for my first band. Around the same time in 1968 , dad bought me my first Baird reel-to-reel quarter track recorder. This, combined with my (loose) understanding of electronics, led me into recording.

I used to sit upstairs in the box room with my best mate, tape recorder, microphone and the two of us would attempt to broadcast a radio show via intercom located upstairs with a wire to a downstairs speaker. My mum would be listening to us whilst ironing.

I started my career in electrical engineering in 1969, passing my City and Guilds Certificate in 1973, with credit mind you.

I loved sound and music (no, not THAT *Sound Of Music*) and when I heard the Small Faces hit' *Itchycoo Park* I had to work out how they'd done that phasing on the drums. This is how I discovered flanging, NO, not that type of flange, but using two tape machines and manually slowing one or the other using the flange of the tape spool. Back then, even sci-fi hadn't thought of the Internet, so trial and error became a good friend.

During my first job in electrical engineering I must have had at least a hundred attempted self-electrocutions, but despite my dedication the company closed four years later, leaving me unemployed.

My father got me into the printing game, and another four years later I at least knew how litho worked!

left the print and at the same time I signed a
three-year music publishing deal, played the
Marquee club London supporting Rock band
UFO in Wardour Street, London , joined Rock
band Sledghammer and had three record releases
by 1980.

Next I travelled to Australia looking for work
mainly in music writing and performing with
singer **Gary Wenzell** and my co-writer **David
Mann** and after six or so weeks realising theirs
no work in music went down the road of trying
to get a job In electrical work.

However by the time I got my City and Guilds
through the post (no email available in 1980) my
visa had run out and so did the money. I decided
after ten weeks of a rock n roll rollercoaster that I
needed to return to the UK.

September 1984 was a good year: I married
Linda and also started my career in sound.
The accounts below are a good indication on how
to do well and how not to do well as a sound
engineer.

All jobs have their ups and downs; in television
you rarely have a "normal" day - boring maybe,

but when things are good they are really good. For instance, you get to meet all sorts of interesting people, from CBeebies' Mr Tumble to the Queen. On other days you could be strapping microphones to **Status Quo**, the cast of Red Dwarf or even bomb disposal engineers about to defuse live armaments!

On the other hand, when you have an annoying director, your kit plays up or the talent acts as if they are the Queen, your days not quite so good…

Fortunately, sound is my hobby and my life outside my family.

Due to some people not wanting to being named, Iv'e missed out some surnames.

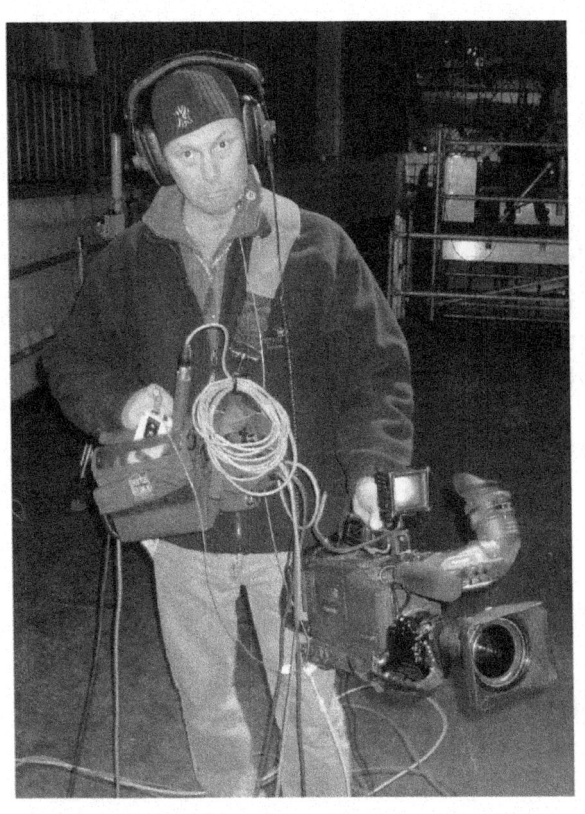

As you can see, I have Camera, Sound, Four wire and ready to go.

Late summer 1983 was my first year in the industry. Having passed two interviews I was offered the job as TO (technical operator) 1 Sound Operator, which meant assisting a great guy.

He was Peter Furney. He was TO3. Technical Operator Level 3 (He was my boss)
.

First Location 1983

Peter Furney showed me the ropes on my first location, where I was introduced to the glamorous side of the industry: an army gym. I stood amongst sweaty squaddies armed with nothing but a fish-pole boom, which had a microphone attached to the far end.

Peter was safely hidden away in a truck round the corner, but kept on running in shouting "Cut!" and letting me know the sound was "Very ambient". Close inspection showed that the mic was pointing at the ceiling…

Second time with Peter was in Manley Manor, working with **Sir Harry Secombe.** I wasn't doing any sound as such then. Now we have these hi-tec radios to talk to each other, Pete doesn't have to run to me anymore.

Filming at Sandhurst involving the Queen, and using an OB truck (Outside Broadcasting) Peter was on mixer, me on doesn't-have-a-clue. I set up the largest boom pole in History for this regal appointment. Thirty foot up (well it seemed that high) stood my boom and it was to pick up general atmos.

That was my job done so I sat in the truck with Peter and relaxed with a cup of tea, really proud of my miking technique. Then all of a sudden I heard a huge bang and some murmurs. "What was that?" I said to Peter. Peter just looked at me. I could see he wasn't happy. You could see in his eyes.

I ran outside, looked left and then right and then thought oh shit. My heavy-duty mic stand had ended up on six or seven ladies' heads. I should have put some weights on the bottom of the stand, so the wind couldn't blow it over. No one complained, which was good.

Pete showed me how a condenser tube cancellation microphone worked.
I said I understood, but for a new boy at 30 years old was embarrassed to ask.
It was in one ear and out the other. Brain cancellation.

Once I'd learnt one end of the microphone from the other, Peter showed me around the sound dubbing suite and how, by doing location sound, you could see what was needed and was not needed for the dub, saving time and making a better-polished product.

Very soon, I was let out on my own. I thought I looked very cool, you know mixer, headphones and boom mic. Oh yes boom mic! Working outside was always a bit embarrassing as the microphone had to be covered with a furry cover (to reduce wind noise) which to everybody in the world would comment "Hows Doogle". Does it really look like "Doogle" out of "The magic roundabout"? Excuse me.

Another great guy was **Johnathan Marks** not only was he the sound supervisor with SSVC (Services Sound and Vision Corporation) but with the help of **John Randall**, Jonathan Marks got me the job.

Jonathan also taught me sound but on top of that, because I've always written and performed music, he wanted me to write some pieces for his drama productions. Jonathan has a lot of energy in his direction. He won quite a few film awards for **SSVC.** Through Jonathan I got to write the **IBA** ident music for channel 3 and 4 which lasted three years thanks to **Bruce Randall**.

I then went on to write many pieces to picture for SSVC, Xerox, Airbus and BFBS TV.

One of the first jobs I did with Jonathan involved a squaddie. He came up to me and said "how sensitive is that microphone"? I was speechless and on top of that embarrassed. Jonathan was very quick on the defence and said "very sensitive"!!

Back in the eighties, before cassettes (let alone hard drives and solid state were invented) professional video was recorded onto inch-wide tape, which was wound onto large spools. The recorder in question was made by a sadist at Ampex, and called a VPR20.

The poor VT operator (**Charlie Dean**) had to carry this really heavy machine around; I had it quite easy then as they employed VT ops. You daren't let the tape run off the end as it took ages to re-lace it backwards with one one-inch spool on top of another, a nightmare.

In 1984 things improved with the Sony camcorder, which used an early professional cassette format called Betacam. It looked the same as the long forgotten Betamax, but its workings were very different.

Cameramen hated this camera because it was backbreaking and about three feet long, so it didn't take long for the recorder back end to be detached and given to the underworked soundman.

I do remember the early days, everyone was out on a job and I had very little knowledge of anything, so when the phone rang in the crew room asking me to bring an HMI 2kw lamp to the roundabout at Chalfont grove, I thought Shit.

I rushed over to the Island to find an open well a very deep well, well I fumbled a lot but managed to fire up the lamp shone it down the hole and that was that ! Then a week later it was filled in. My only job in lighting.

SAS Hereford and Brecon Beacons 1984

This was a fantastic experience; my one and only sound assistant job for a freelance film crew, where I learned all about the Narga 4s stereo tape recorder and proper boom swinging.

It started when I had to drive our lighting van plus generator down to an SAS base in Hereford. I had no knowledge of driving a van let alone with a generator on the back. All went well until, when I arrived I couldn't reverse the damn thing, I had to reverse into a small parking slot, left went right, right went left and I made a right pig's ear of it.

Then appeared a SAS soldier who said "leave it to me ". Fucking know alls - should stick to storming embassies.

It was great filming in Hereford, with guys jumping out of Scout helicopters 100ft above your head, adrenalin flowing and a couple of them hurt themselves abseiling out of the helicopters.

Then we headed off to the Welsh countryside of Brecon. Army Stores was the location and

followed the elite force up Pen-e- fan, a large hill, sorry a small mountain.
The weather was awful, and with 100 mph winds it was bloody cold.

I remember I needed to have a leak, so I put all my kit down, got my old chap out and started to wee. I got soaked and then realising I was facing the wrong way, quickly turned into the wind and to my amazement my flow of urine went for about a mile, just missing other hill climbers.

But the day was spoilt when two SAS guys were blown over one of the ridges and died.

The Falkland tour November 1984

We were sent to the Falklands in '84 to do a "Welcome to the Falklands" briefing video with **John Randall** on camera, **Chris W** directing and me on Sound/VT 30 hours, the journey took in total.
The first leg to Ascension was in a Tri-Star with seats facing backwards. (felt like I was going home) no luck. It took around 15 hours, and then we stayed overnight in a room filled with 22 bunk beds .

We went straight to the bar and got trolleyed just to get a good night's sleep. The place was disgusting, filled with farting, smelly socks and vomiting. And that was just JR … only joking.

In the morning we continued our journey to Stanley Airport. A Hercules C120 was awaiting us. On boarding we noticed there wasn't an air hostess but a load master. We had to sit on paratroopers' seats with everyone's luggage strapped to the middle of the fuselage.

There was no leg room. We had to put our feet up on the cases. Luckily mum had given me some sleeping tablets. I remember sleeping for three hours, waking up and then JR would say "listen to this", playing his Monty Python cassette, having a laugh and popping another pill and back to sleep.

I couldn't believe it: On arrival at Stanley airfield and after the initial briefing we were shown a coloured picture of a hand blown apart and told where not to walk and also to look out for mine field signs.
Within two hours we were back in the skies on a reconnaissance flight which lasted another four hours. The pilot thought it was funny to fly 100 odd feet above the South Atlantic Ocean and then pull 4Gs, sort of vertical, in a Hercules. Bastard!

Well I thought this was the end! And as I dropped my mixer and my face, we fell out of the air, so we're now floating on negative G's.

I was dying, my mixer broke, I heard 1k tone from my mixer and that was that. Felt like crap, everything broken, but three hours later we were in the RAF engineering workshop at Stanley, repairing the SQN mixer.

We poor soundmen still had to lug the arse end of the camera about, and for this tour my multitasking was tested to the limit. I carried and worked the mics, radio packs, booms, the arse end of the camera (recorder, remember) and a neat sound mixer called an SQN.

In addition to this, because I had the camera's rump, I had to log the shots using time code, which is a series of long numbers, each one unique to each single frame of video. Luckily for me, I just had to note down the start and finish number of each shot! Sometimes the cameraman would be connected to the VT machine with a thick umbilical cable.

The cameraman could hit the record button on the camera whenever he wanted to, which was often without telling me. If I were paying attention I'd feel the machine running, frantically noting the start time code and moving the boom to get the mic in position.

By the time I got the mic into position he or she would often stop recording, which led to interesting conversations between us. This was the frustrating side of it…not mentioning any names JP.

Walking in my own footsteps in a minefield seemed the way to go, I thought it would be safe but the bomb disposal guy told me later you should always walk on fresh sand because it reduces pressure on the sand,

Shit, phew! Poop +/?

We did many locations on the West and the East Falkland Islands. As there were no roads it was a lot of walking, Land Rover and helicopter.
The Bristow transporter I remember very well, a very noisy chopper with a very loud load master, they used these on the oil rigs. I remember this guy looking very concerned. Apparently he had found a tiny screw and was trying to locate where it had come from.

It was only on departing 10 minutes later I realised one of the screws from my 12V T powered box had come adrift. I don't know from his reactions if he wanted to punch me or it was a sigh of relief.

Stanley to Mount Pleasant track – yes, track; this was 1984. This bumpy ride was just the beginning of a memorable three weeks.

All of a sudden I saw a flash to my left. I was sitting in the back of an Army Land Rover bouncing all over the place and slowly fixed my eyes into the field.

And to my amazement and also horror, I saw that a cow had trodden on a mine and blown its lower leg off and it fell to the ground.
But we couldn't stop or even think about phoning help. Come to think about it, we didn't have mobiles in 1984.

Nevertheless, imagine standing in the cold, not having washed for a week, in the same, unwashed clothes you'd been wearing since you arrived, making sure the microphones were pointing in the right directions, their levels were right, jotting down timecode and , most importantly, remembering to press "record". At least the sheep were impressed!

Here are some pics of one of my first shoots I did with Sir Harry Secombe in 1983. I was Peters apprentice so learning the radio walkie talkie and the basic sound ropes was my job.

Also below is pics of the great blues singer, harp player and radio presenter Paul Jones. Great guy and a pleasure to work with.

Paul was also was the lead singer of the sixties pop group Manfred Man and The blues Band.

Paul worked in our studio two promoting CD's For "Timeline" A company promoting music CD's

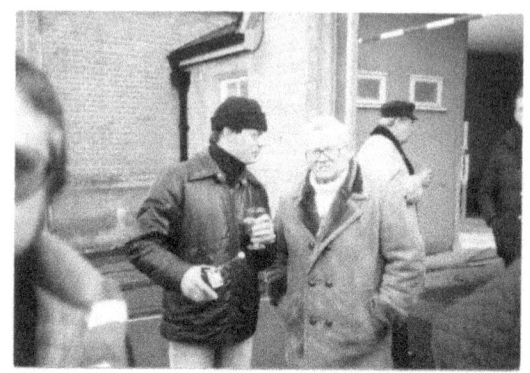

Harry Secombe

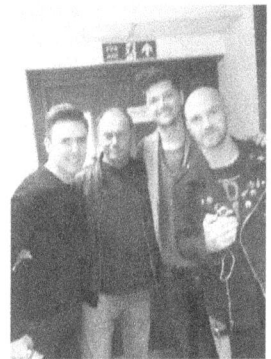

The Script

Melton Mowbray Dog Training

Two weeks filming in Melton Mowbray with the dog handling team was interesting. In some down time I dressed up in the dog training equipment, you know the padding and stuff with a silly cage on your head then having to run away from a massive Alsatian and be floored was to say the least scary.

Bill Brackley, our driver-grip-spark was minding his own business on the dog handling coarse at Melton Mowbray with the SAS when a large Alsatian dog decided to take a piece out of his side.
Poor old Bill was rushed to hospital , they got him there in four minutes in one of their elite Range Rovers only to be sitting in A & E for four hours to be seen to. Bill still has a bad scar.

Fred Harris

(BBC Playschool) was one of our children's presenters from the early 80s and only stopped presenting with BFBS around 2009 due to cut backs.

The first job I did with Fred was in Dixons, Uxbridge. It must have been around 1984.

This was a piece to camera (on a camera track), with Fred talking about science, maths, formulas - his forte.

We finished filming around 11pm only to find we had been locked in. We were underground and all the shutters were down and locked. It took us hours to get the authorities to open the shutters and let us out.

Fred has this technique of making his voice sound "one legged", that is, squeaky, very thin. Very annoying at first, but when you've known Fred that long you accept his humour. It's great for winding up engineers.

Fred was another **Roy Castle** in the way he could play loads of different musical instruments so, it was just another brilliant day when **Ben Castle**, **Roy Castle's** son, came on the show, a sax player and a great guy. Fred loved it; you know, Fred has over 16 saxophones in his collection.

Strike Command, Wycombe, Bucks

Our Boss **David Goldsmith** sent John Randall, Peter Furney and my good self to a field opposite RAF Strike Command, High Wycombe to film the last fly-past of the Vulcan bomber.
We arrived at 10 am set up and ready to roll for a 12.30 flypast.We then found out it would be delayed until 1500hrs.

Now just up the road from strike command is a nice pub and after a few pints and a few hours we arrived back in the field, stuck the camera out of the roof facing southeast, as we'd been told, mics standing by, and waited.

After 20 minutes of suspense we heard the roar of the bomber, which flew south to west so we missed the whole thing. I think John panned really quickly and just caught the wing. We got a bit of a telling off when we returned to base, but it wasn't our fault.

Filming in tanks was very interesting, but a very dangerous area to work in. Whilst the warrior tank I was on was stationary, I had time to place microphones within the cab area , even then you would bang your head on something or other.

Happy with audio levels, I relocated myself at the back of the vehicle with the VPR50, mixer, gun mic and only two arms. Then the idiot driver decided to floor it, every bump, dip, on the range shook and took the recorded let alone myself all over the shop. Two foot off the floor. We nearly lost the recorder. We nearly lost me!

Back home, things were about to get even heavier with the introduction of the Sony BVW25 (Betacam SP) recorder, which offered higher quality than the original Betacam.

At this point the cassettes were, as mentioned, the same size as a domestic Betamax, but would only record for a maximum of 20 minutes.

Later came the BVW50, which was heavier and took a larger Betacam SP cassette format, which allowed us a whole 90 minutes of recording time and off-tape monitoring. Hooray!!

.
The by now overloaded sound operator now had to carry a BVW50, a SQN 4S, a mic system and logging system!! And with my forth arm attach a radio mic.

Bad year! Can't wait for the pro camcorder to arrive or it's back to film.

Sound dubbing

The sound dubbing suite was called SYPHER **SY**ncronize **P**ost **H**ouse **E**ight track **R**ecorder. This was labelled on the door. I know, it took me a few months to explain to clients what it meant.

I would say Sypher. Err sound err post house (I remembered that bit) something or other. Anyway months later I learnt it and then shortly afterwards we purchased a 16 track two inch so that would have been **SYPHSR** - bizarre!

This was a great experience. Working with time code was quite hard for me as I'm a bit dyslexic with numbers and nerve racking sometimes with producers looking over your shoulder.

It was the waiting game. When I say waiting I don't mean waiting for the client to turn up, or waiting for the tea to arrive I was waiting for the Voice Over ¼ inch reel to reel to catch up with the two-inch master tape just to drop a five-second voice-over line in and then it didn't happen because it hadn't synchronized in the 10-second pre roll, frustrating not to say embarrassing. AHHH!!

One of my first jobs in sound dubbing was doing a voice over recording. You know: make it simple for the apprentice. I was hoping for someone less famous to start with but broadcaster **Jan** came in, and after a 10-minute script check she said she was ready.

Now the Soundcraft 24/4/2 1980s mixing desk had a button called "talkback". This button enables me to talk to the VO (voice over) booth. So here I go. I started the Studer reel-to-reel in record mode, pressed the button to tell Jan to speak in her own time, but half an inch away from the T/B button is a 1K oscillator,(line up tone)

 I can still see Jan's face to this day.

I actually heard it through the triple glazed window. It must have been around 10 watts in her ears. Sorry, Jan.

I had an internal call from a guy called Ken, a film editor who worked on the first floor. He asked if I could find a sound effect for him. He was one of those old-school grumpy white hair types.

I said okay and spent fifteen minutes looking through the library when Peter Furney came in. He said "How's it going Clint?", I replied, "That old fucker upstairs wants a tank sound effect and I can't find one anywhere." As I said that I caught a reflection of him standing behind me in the TV monitor.

 Ken had only followed me down stairs to the duding suite. He heard everything!! You've heard the term "crawl into a corner and die".

I loved dubbing a series for **Meridian TV** called *Coastline* with **Jack Pizzey.**

The editor (whose name was **Harry Amos**) sat with me on the dub and we just made it work. The recorded sound was from the camera mic left and radio mic right. It took a lot of jiggery pokery to make it sound "acceptable stereo", using stereo wide and other shit. And then after all that the programme was transmitted in MONO!!!!

Again doing loads of location recordings helped me realise what was needed in the sound-dubbing suite – sorry, SYPHER!!!

Our newer Sound Dubbing Suite (not called Sypher) used digital technology: a Neve Logic 1.

BBC
Engineering Training Department

This is to certify that

Mr. C. Nurse

has attended formal courses at
The BBC Engineering Training Centre
Wood Norton, Evesham, England,
in accordance with the following schedule.

Q Television Sound Operations Course

on

24th March - 23rd April 1986

A.G. Owen
PhD, CEng. M.I.E.E.
Head of Engineering Training Department

T.B. McCrirrick
C.Eng. F.I.E.E. F.I.E.R.E. F.R.T.S.
Director of Engineering

I was offered scripts from **Clive Mitchell**
(Producer/Director) and declined as I thought it
would be easier to follow someone's dialogue
and log it phonetically
All seemed well until the commentator asked to
be dropped in after the word ...feo..or fandeo..or
.....Italians always end everything with "o".

German was the easiest.

Not such a good prank

After a long three weeks of dubbing and using
five different languages and very exhausted, I
thought I would end Friday night with a prank.

I loaded a CD of horror music into the system
and looped it, then saved it on the hard drive.
Playing back I had the flying faders moving
slowly and then all the faders thrust up for a
horror stab. I then turned the air conditioning on
full cold and set a spotlight on the moving faders.

This looked and sounded very spooky and I
thought if I left this running all weekend anyone
entering the dubbing suite would shit themselves.

I forgot about the cleaner .... we didn't see her
again. Sorry.

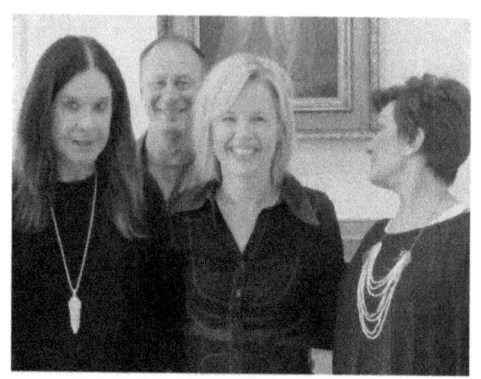

Ozzy Osbourne, me , Sara Burls , Sharon Osbourne

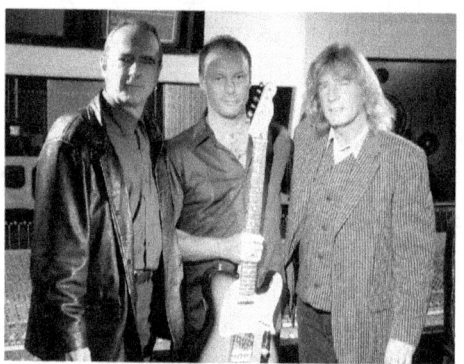

Status Quo

Iraq conflict film 1993

This year we travelled to America with **Jonathan Marks** and **Tim Hore** to interview American military leaders regarding the 1991 gulf war. First stop was South Carolina and we spent two days there waiting for our kit to be released from customs (wrong paperwork) or something before we interviewed **Stormin' Norman**.

Once sorted we headed off to New York to the Pentagon to interview **General Franks.**That went well, so we then drove as near as we could to get to the White House just to get the best shot. After walking across a vast green area with all the kit, we set up set up the camera.

A policeman approached us and told us not to film here I said we'd just been filming in the Pentagon. He said "Where?" I said "The Pentagon.", he said "Where?" "The Peenagon, Penagoon" five accents and five minutes later,. he turned to me and said "You mean the Pentagon". Good grief.

Horror

Yvette Fielding presenter of *Most Haunted* used to present for BFBS Room 785 (children's channel) run by **Sharron Hollins** and **Liz Pennes.**

This lovely lady had a habit of swearing, which was so funny and so close to "on air".

One day before going on air JR said to Yvette "Did you know studio 2 was haunted?" She said "Show me." Beforehand JR had lowered the temperature of the studio.

I rushed down ahead of the couple, ran onto the studio floor, donned the old man's mask and hid under some black drape in the corner of the floor, trying not to breathe heavily. I could hear Yvette and JR enter the studio and these are the words I heard from JR: "This studio is haunted. Can you feel the cold?" She said "Oh yes!" JR said "If you walk down the back end you get a really weird feeling." At this point she was about six feet away from me. I just stood up and screamed. Can you imagine: old man's mask in a spot light?"

Yvette just screamed. Phew!! My heart was pumping.

Westbury , Wiltshire

Alan Frost was the director, we were filming on Salisbury plain and staying in Westbury. Ken the landlord told us of the story about the grey lady who use to haunt the bar. She came from the gents toilet down the hallway and behind the bar and then disappeared.

Anyway one evening after filming we ended up in the bar, Alan did a spoof interview with Ken and I gave Alan a handheld mic set the video into record and disappeared into the toilet to change into my 'scare the shit outta ken' mask and hood. Whilst waiting for my cue I did look a little strange in the full length mirror in the gents.

JR put the shits up me by knocking on the public bar wall which leads to - you guessed it - the toilet. Anyway the interview was recorded with me in the background all masked up and I think Ken still thinks on playback it was the grey lady.

Always take your key

It happened in a Salisbury plain hotel, I can't remember the job.

My hotel room had an inner door and an outer door ,which led to the hallway with a short passage way between them.

I Woke up at three in the morning in my Birthday suite to go to the toilet, I opened the door and then closed it thinking the loo was in the hallway then as I opened the second door realised I was in the hallway...starker's.

Panicking I tried to get back in to my room but to no avail , it was in the early hours of the morning so making sure no one was around I crept down the hotel stairs holding my tackle , got to reception area and noticed their was a low voltage security light behind the desk.
On close inspection, I could see the spare key in my room pigeonhole box, so I grabbed it legged it up stairs and no body saw me phew!

London Dungeons was a laugh (not) with **Simeon Courtie** and **Emma Dixon** (Lee)
We were only allowed to film before 10am, that's when the public are allowed in, for health and safety reasons.

Sharron Hollins and **Mark Gosling** went on a recce. **Omar N'Jie (** Production Assistant**)** and myself were waiting ages in a dingy dungeon for them to return. I said to Omar I'll go and look for them, now can you imagine this? It's pitch black, smells of rats' piss and just then the public address system came on playing haunting music and manic laughing.

As you guessed I got lost, very scary. Later when I asked the tour guide about four skeletons hanging on the dungeon wall he said that the first one was real and it was donated to the London Dungeons around one hundred years ago. Talking of skeletons, Bill Brackley reminded me of a shoot we did in the Queens Elizabeth Hospital ,Woolwich, London.
having a laugh in some down time. I decided to scare everyone with this skeleton ,
Then the nurse came in and said "can you put him down please" apparently it was real.

Sharron Hollins also reminded me recently about a shoot we did in Lapland with Santa. Apparently, we had finished filming a piece with him and I heard Santa (St Nicholas) say in broken English "*Sharron, when I come to England I must take you out for dinner.*" On hearing this in my closed back headphones I shouted "Fucking hell,

Santa's just pulled Sharron!" Didn't realise I was shouting.

Later, waiting for Santa to arrive, we all went for a stroll and round the back of a hut and saw a clear bag full of reindeer heads and bright red blood in the snow, so shocked by the fact a kid might wander around the back and catch a glimpse, I questioned Mr Santa Claus about this issue. He had no answer.

Later on in the grotto

I asked Santa to do a request to camera. **Debbie Flint's promo** was good. Sharron's was good, but Santa said "Sasha and Lauren". My daughters' names are Sasha and Laurie.
Do you think he was getting his own back?

Debbie did a lot with Room 785 , she also promoted my daughters pop video for BLISS Baby Life Support Systems,We went to Lapland and had a good laugh on the skidoos, my fish pole managed to snap in half with the cold

Around this time we had a new boss (sound supervisor) **Ray Bell ,** I got on well with Ray I think because he was not only a decent bloke But he was an inside based guy and taught me loads about studio techniques .

When **Room 785** first broadcast we ran a programme with a witch called Wizadora. Every time she waved her wand you had this sparkly sound effect with the visuals.

I had a similar sound effect on my cart machine, so when boredom set in I would play some added wizard noise. As you can imagine after a few months it got out of hand and I was prompted by Sharron (the Producer/Director and vision mixer) Hollins to play this effect even when Wizadora hadn't waved her wand.

The funny thing is I don't think anyone noticed.

We did this show live every day. **Richard Orford** was our presenter that afternoon but failed to turn up. After ringing him to see where he was, he decided to do the opening link via his cell phone. We put a slide up mixed with his audio, job done. He was explaining to the audience how he was stuck in traffic.

This day was a laugh! **Jane Farnham** presented the kids show live. We used to get emails from all over the world wishing kiddies happy birthdays. Jane read out this email "And it's a happy birthday to Sarah, much love from Phil

Mcgroin." Well we just pissed ourselves. What made it worse she did the same again in the next link -"Happy Birthday from Pat McCrack" - and she didn't even register. We found out later it was the oil rig workers who had picked up our satellite signal and just having a joke.

Getting teas and coffee with **Sharron Hollins** for the gallery crew, this was before we had runners. Anyway in reception we were just about to come back to the studio and then noticed on TX output monitor the end credits of our preceding programme. Trying to get through the security door with our fobs, we only had seconds to get to the gallery. My coffee was dropped in the rush. I managed to get to the mixer and push the fader up on the 10 second count. Phew, just in the nick of time!

On the Queen mum's 100th Birthday, Room 785 did a TV special. Instead of me doing studio sound I had to stand in the wings and every time presenter Simeon Courtie said the words "The Queen Mother" I would play a fanfare on the bugle. I was rubbish at doing this as I hadn't played the bugle for at least 40 years with the Boys Brigade.

The deal was done that I wouldn't be seen. Little did I know a second camera was always facing me and Sharron would cut up that camera live.

They made me a DVD to take home the next day. "Bastards".

Tim Dixon also presented Room 785 and one afternoon on a live show, I showed him my police handcuffs that I had just purchased on ebay. We had around five minutes to go before going on air.

I thought it funny to handcuff Tim to the chair, all seemed quite funny until a minute to air I couldn't open the cuffs, they had rusted inside. Tim did the first link with handcuffs on . I later added some WD 40 and all was good.

Studio Two featuring the sports presenter **Murray**.

I had to record a voiceover with Murray. We had a voiceover booth where you couldn't see the artist, in other words there was no window. So I set up the mic on the table, as usual it all sounded good. I gave him a talkback feed and that was that. he sounded great. "Ok Murray, I am recording" and he sounded rubbish, very ambient and well off mic.

I went into the commentary booth , and he was standing up, giving it everything he had. Can you imagine? The U87 was about three foot below his mouth. Facing his groin. … No not Pat McGroin.

Things got a little worse when later we had to do some tracking shots in the studio.
I took the radio mic in and for a joke said to Murray "I've come to mic you up", but I had a massive Neumann U87 mic in my hand. He didn't think that funny, so I put the lapel radio mic on him and that was that. I thought I must grow up.
 This way I didn't care if he sat down, stood up, lay down - he wouldn't be "off mic". We had a break and after 15 minutes went back onto the studio floor. This time I took some Murray mints.

I offered one to the highly acclaimed sports presenter, saying "Would you like a Murray mint, Murray?" There was a long pause and he didn't answer. If looks could kill … I gave up after that.

 Pauline Quirke turned up on a Sunday to do some voice-overs for a Channel 5 jobby. She loved coming to our studios because she only lived five miles away. First thing she asked "Where can I have a cigarette, Clint?" I led her to the so-called green room while I sorted out the time coded DAT machine. What a lovely and friendly person!

SFX (sound effects)

The best wind sound effect I ever got was in Norway: winds of only around 50 miles per hour against a flagpole. Remember, you cannot hear wind; it's only when it hits something. Preferably not the mic. You knew that.

I remember doing a location drama and the shot was actor **Jack McKenzie** talking to camera in an office. In the background a bus passed by. You didn't hear it (so what?) normally. If you heard it they would do a retake, so it sounded good to me. When it went to dubbing the producer said to me "Can you add a bus sound to that shot?" I looked at him in that way: "What the fuck?"

So picking up my location kit I headed down to Seer Green, Bucks, only two miles from where I was working where I knew was a quiet green bus route, saw a bus in front of me, overtook it in my very not fast Ford Sierra, put my foot down,

screeched to a halt, legged it out, stood like idiot in front of someone's garden, pointed the 416 mic and as the bus passed... the man in the garden started his petrol lawn mower up.
This is why I now have a big sound effects library.

Looking bemused and it seemed like hours... I only waited 20 minutes for another one to come along. Result: this had now taken me an hour to record a bus "up and pass", a soundman's term for an object approaching and then going away again..

I hate it when a producer/director or even the presenter asks, have you got a sound we can use for the programme literally seconds before going on air. Yeh, I've got loads of time. We have a CD library, but try and find the effect in ten minutes, and if you can then by the time you get back to the studio it's too late.

Today I have well over 18,800 SFX in my iphone library (sad). I can get an effect, transfer and playback in 15 seconds, but some flash arse always catches me out with an effect I haven't got.

Norway (cover pic) taken by *Charlie Deane*
sunrise 10am sunset 3pm

Carrying a BVW 50 / mixer under 2 tons of army
overcoats is quite challenging.
Director says "Run to record, soundman, eer I
think so yes mm," and so on. I can recall taken
the cable ties off of the BNC coaxials in -32C
and the cables just stayed curled.
When you tried to straighten them they snapped.
Another hint in sub zero temperatures: don't
breathe through your nose quickly - it will freeze
up.

We left the hotel and travelled out of the town of
Voss , which was quite difficult as the night
before vehicles had left tyre grooves in the snow
and they had now frozen. I'm driving in eight
inch tram lines, unable to steer, which was quite
frightening, especially when a lorry is travelling
towards you.

I think the temperature the next day was -17. The
sun was out and a helicopter was landing. I took
my gloves off to govern the levels on the mixer,
which turned out to be a very silly thing. The
wind chill off of the rotor blades hitting the snow
then hitting us was horrendous... I managed to
get sick with mild frostbite. Not nice. Luckily the
army guy soon got me back on my legs again.

Walking down town in **Voss** , Norway to the pub I think was called the Railway, which had this miniature train track all around the restaurant. As you ate your dinner this train would start and stop above your head, good idea but very off putting. Jon Poynter loves this. He loved his trains.

The next evening the temperature was -20.

So walking down the hill to the Railway pub with Charlie and Jon with three girls walking towards us, I farted, not loud but these girls fell over laughing, I thought there's no way they heard that, then thinking they were laughing at someone behind me, looked around and no one was there it was only then realised when I farted I left a massive fart cloud in the air.

We did another film in Norway, working title *Driving in Norway*, a great shoot for three weeks. **Jon** ploughed our camera platform Range Rover into an army Land Rover, and then later we filmed a Scimitar tank do an up and pass, then out of shot and "BANG", we walked around the corner and flipping heck because of the tank the rear end of the Range Rover was gone. But apart from that the two-week shoot went well.

I remember we were filming a presenter walking and talking in the snow'this was a piece to camera' The cameraman, lighting and director were all trying to walk in unison with the presenter, just so as we didn't hear loads of feet. (icy snow is very noisy)

The director Chris Wilson later that week went home sick but asked the crew to cover some mortar firing shots for another programme. We said okay. Next morning **Jon** , **Charlie Dean** and I sat around the breakfast table thinking should we do it? and after half an hour or so later Jon decided not to do the footage. Just as well. In the area we were to film three died when a mortar exploded.

Skiing in Norway

Mark Hearn and myself. Mark had grown a "Terry Waite" beard. I suppose this kept him warm in the sub minus temperatures. Mark and I had to share a room as I think Jonathon Marks had a problem with our previously booked hotel. I had a razor and that evening I said to Mark "that beard looks hideous. shall I shave it off?" Mark was in a similar state as me and said "yes", blunt razor and all.

Mark woke up the next morning with thick and far between tufts of beard on his face and blood all down his neck. Funny at breakfast the next morning,

More Norway

Another Norway job we did in the eighties was 'Allied Command Europe Mobile Force'. ACE Mobile Force for short.

 We stayed at a hotel in Voss; we were filming paratroopers landing on the frozen lake behind the hotel which involved European, British and American troops.

Our evening entertainment at the hotel was a five piece band, two girl's singers and a load of weird looking bearded guys on drums, guitars and keyboards. I actually bought their cassette album they sounded a bit like Abba.

After a couple of days filming we would watch the rushes back in the hotels dinning hall when no one was around.

One afternoon whilst checking our weeks footage the band were rehearsing on the stage , then you would get one then two then three of the band members sit themselves behind us intrigued at what we were watching.

Any way two weeks later back at Chalfont we were separately interviewed by secret squirrels, we were later told they were spies!!!

Back at the hotel we would check out what beer the hotel sold, made a note, went to the NAFFI the next day and bought four crates of lager for a tenth of the price.

We would walk through reception with all these bottles in camera bags, flight cases etc. then having to go back out to get the cameras and bits in. you could hear the beer bottles rattling in the camera bag.

Director **Chris W**. made us laugh; to chill his bottles of beer , he would hang them outside his hotel room window on a piece of string .

Forgetting to take them in that evening he would wake the next morning to find the bottles has smashed with the cold leaving frozen beer dangling from a piece of string; well it was minus 30 degrees outside

It was just under the three week shoot in Norway when on the last night of the shoot the Colonel (technical advisor) asked me if he could borrow my room as he had just pulled a Norwegian lass, I mean dog.

I didn't want to but after a few beers I let him, now beers from the NAFFI were thirty pence instead of the three pounds at the bar. So we sank a few.

An hour and a half later the colonel came back into the bar with my room keys, I was relieved to know I wasn't going to sleep in the bar.

Anyway on entering my room in the early hours I couldn't believe my eyes.

They had left stains all over my bed, couch and all up the wall I thought WTF.
I should have slept in the bar.

On telling the crew the next morning they all fell about laughing.

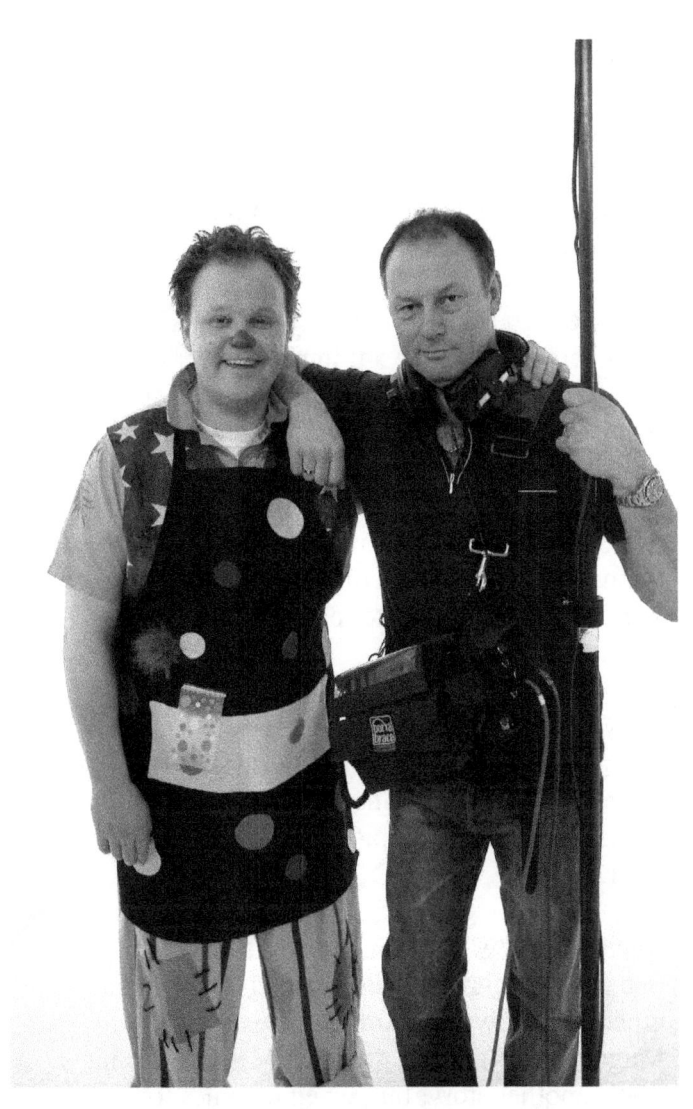

Northern Ireland

This was scarier than the Falklands, in the sense there's no control in NI. Stones thrown by kids and thumbs up the next minute. You don't know who likes you or not.

Interviewing a soldier whose mate got killed two days before was quite a traumatic experience. I was so interested in what he had to tell I nearly lost it and dropped the boom into shot.

I'll never forget we were picked up at Belfast airport, put in a white van, with whited-out windows with a little scrape hole in the back window, and was told to look out for anything suspicious.

Very exciting but later we changed to a car. A few miles down the road the corporal stopped to get petrol and handed me his Browning 9mm HP35 semi-automatic pistol and told me to "look after it "

Luckily I knew this gun very well as I had owned one of these guns and also belonged to a rifle club. I even owned a Smith & Wesson 357 Magnum - you know: "MAKE MY DAY", but that's another story, but, when it comes to the real thing, adrenalin kicks in. It was quite frightening to say the least. He returned and I reluctantly gave the gun back. But the Dunblane massacre finished off my firearms hobby. All my guns were handed in to Feltham police station.

BBC Evesham

Three years passed and then in 1986 I attended the BBC Engineering Training Department near Evesham and passed my formal television course.

This was a good experience. I had a great time, down the pub every night. Some of the other classmates were drinking vodka till 3am it's a wonder we got anything done. I didn't learn any more about sound dubbing or location than I already knew.

However I did learn a lot about studios which at that time I didn't really want to get into, I preferred location and sound dubbing. It was a shame I had a shit car because my brakes had gone and I lived 100 miles from Evesham.

After the second week, some bastard at a tyre company in Harrow Weald had stuck a screwdriver through a shroud on the back of my brakes, pissing oil everywhere that cost me three hours and loads of money I didn't have. This also made me late for Evesham.

Anyway after all that and having a great time with some really nice guys, we produced a pop video , now on YouTube. Check out **Clint Nurse** and you will see it. Anyway I have the BBC certificate on my studio wall.

First "Film" shoot

My first stint of recording sound for film was with the Navy.I will never forget filming a (RAS), Replenishment at sea, that is refuelling a Royal Navy Destroyer from a RFA (Royal Fleet Auxiliary) tanker , we were at sea for over three weeks.

All the camera gear was sent to HMS Gloucester… ARRI 16mm, Nagra Stereo tape recorder. Two weeks before the shoot, the equipment was shipped to America, and then loaded onto a destroyer moored up in San Francisco which was to sail eventually to West Palm Beach through the Panama Canal.

The only kit I couldn't send was my headphones, as I needed them for other jobs.
so I decided to take then with me on the plane.

We arrived on the West Coast and spent three days enjoying the sun, bars etc, not worrying about anything. I had a drink with the cameraman **Bob H,** who said he knew my dad in the RAF during the war. Wow! Another whiskey!!

The morning we boarded the ship I realised I had forgotten my personal headphones and much needed 24 D type batteries for the Nagra tape recorder.

Panicking, I asked the unit manager if he could rush down town to get some batteries. He came back with only twelve, but luckily they lasted. This worked as I had a mains supply on the ship to run my Nagra. Logging of tapes was done in the evening.

But the headphones were my worst nightmare. The radio comms guy on the bridge lent me a pair of Bakelite headsets. God they hurt, putting pressure on the bony parts of the ear tip. I always carry two sets of headphones now. Oh, and a soldering iron.

Missed a bit here. The first week on board the ship all seven of us slept in one room.

Snoring cameraman downed 22 (miniature) bottles of free whiskey from the plane, who after a couple of weeks fell out a bunk and broke his ribs. Producer/cameraman **Malcolm** took over for the last week.

Oh, the second week, I got to sharing with an officer on opposite bunk beds. I thought it a little weird when I found nude magazines under my bunk bed, but it didn't bother me.

 However, during the afternoon when we had a hurricane up front we decided to called it a day, ship distressed and glasses and plates smashing, I went to my cabin to log my recordings ,and pulled the curtain only to see the officer I'd been sharing with masturbating in the sink! He didn't see me, I quickly retreated.

Drinks on board were 10p a double, so I persevered!

Being "film" and not "video", I wasn't connected to the camera. This was a brilliant idea, except when I looked up after checking my recording the camera crew had disappeared to the next location. It was embarrassing to ask a warrant officer where the crew went.

The Royal Navy RAS 2

The Second RAS was just as before: film again, but the cameraman was **Richard H** and **Steve D** and it was produced and directed by **Malcolm**.

This location was more exotic: Dubai for two days. Set sail down the arse end of Saudi, go left underneath and then up the Red Sea. Then we saw dolphins. They were amazing. The sea was like silk and so calm.

On board was focus puller **Nick W**, showing off his Rolex watch and by proving it was real by placing it in my quadruple whisky. I don't think he ever took that watch off, so you can imagine my whiskey got very cloudy.

The crew said "go and get your fake Rolex Clint". I bought it in Dubai for $25. I rushed back to my cabin and strapped on my Lorex, sorry Rolex, slammed the door shut and trapped my wrist in the door slider thing. And that was that! Second-hand flew off, the black face peeled away and the strap broke.
I got to the bar and told them what I had done and Malcolm proceeded to hit my watch on the bar until the insides fell apart. I thought, this guy's days are numbered.

Arrived in Port Said, Egypt by landing craft about 1.30 in the morning. Some money was exchanged and we had armed escort to Cairo, about 30 miles away down a very dark road, as I remember. The armed escort of seven soldiers with AK47s disappeared after about 500 yards.

We had been told not to stop for anyone. Excuse me, there were six of us in the people carrier with an Egyptian driver who couldn't speak English.

As you might have guessed at around two in the morning we were overtaken by an Egyptian who slowed down, drove parallel with us and then shouted at our driver .

We pulled over, thinking this is it, we're dead. A few shouted words were exchanged, we all sat in silence whispering the obvious and five minutes later we carried on. Phew!

Anyway, we arrived at the hotel in Cairo at 3am with 12 flight cases and around 150 people waiting to check in. I couldn't believe my eyes when **Omar Sharif** with three bodyguards walked past me!
Oh well we were all exhausted by the time the unit manager finally checked us all in.

What an end to a memorable shoot!

Radio mics

We were filming around America/Panama on board a warship that was on active duty i.e. fully equipped with missiles and scanning for pirates etc.

The WO (warrant officer), a part time actor was in a rotten mood. I remember him calling the Captain a C... several times.
After 10 minutes or so an officer on the bridge starts shouting my way, so I walk up under the bridge.

He says they are scanning all frequencies and he told me he could hear the WO swearing so I said "Okay, I'll sort it." I rushed back to the WO, unplugged my receiver and said "You must stop calling the Captain a C...."

Warrant Officer said "Well he is a C..." Just as he said that the Officer appeared again on the bridge, red-faced, screaming down at me again. He said "We all heard that." I said "You can't have heard that - I unplugged the receiver."
, Slight pause. Oh shit, I should have turned off the TRANSMITTER! The Captain was not amused.
The RAS Navy shots we missed due to the three hurricanes we had on the west Mexico seas had to be reproduced at Plymouth Navy base

It was decided to re enact the RAS
(replenishment at sea) at Plymouth.

A Sunday was chosen, as it was quiet. How
wrong could that day have been? Because the
simulator ship is built on concrete we had to
shoot uphill, I know that's not a technical term,
but I think you get the gist.

Who didn't tell us there was a golf course over
the back? Great!! Imagine the scene:
.........Captain... giving orders ...then you see a
bloke in the background with his golf club in
hand and not to mention a caddie.

Anyway after re-angling the camera we started
shooting. Again the WO on the bridge had a way
with words. I put a radio mic on him and let him
go, bad move. He went to the bridge area and
proceeded to f and blind and it wasn't mild.

An hour passed and we were told to stop filming
as there were VIPs passing, so we stopped, saw
some flashy cars and some funny flags on
bonnets, waited 10 and carried on.

15 minutes later a royal type car approaches. A
man runs out, shouts "KILL THE RADIO MIC!"
Apparently the WO and his swearing antics were

broadcast all over the parade ground, on which their were over 200 women and children.

The Royal Tournament, Earls Court

I remember filming the Royal Tournament at Earls Court with the cameraman, director and me running around getting all tangled up in the BNC cable. It must have looked so funny to the spectators, but not me, so the next time we did the Royal Tournament I thought I would be clever.

I aimed a 416 at the Public Address system and radioed that back to my Nargra. By the way, I was standing in the wings out of mischief's way and hard wired an effects mic to the other channel. Job done - or not in this case.

I was monitoring off tape and so thinking "if I can hear it, it's there stuck on the tape". WRONG! Because it was very dark where I was standing , I felt very comfortable , no cables tangled around me and I could monitor the sound out of the hustle and bustle of the crowd..

So, proud of my set up, I started to look around the audience with a smile on my face until to my horror I spotted a guy sitting three feet away from me who was staring at the ground then looking up at me, then staring at the ground then looking at the Nargra.

I looked down in the darkness and noticed the lid had opened on the reel-to-reel, which was dumping the tape all over the floor.

It was most embarrassing, and without a torch I couldn't see what I was doing but later managed to retrieve the tape in Sound Dubbing.

Convoy Cock-up

Catterick Garrison also reminds me of things that can easily go wrong. We were filming a convoy of around 80 vehicles in the woods.
So that our filming vehicles would not be in shot, I drove our Transits to a nearby field. As I entered the field one of the Transits went down an incline, buckling the back ramp, and then got stuck in the mud.

Not too much of a hurry back because I had a gun mic on a stand and the cameraman was operating the BVW50 and levels were set.

I got back to where the cameras were waiting to turnover when the officer in one of the cars wanted to know how to use the flasher, so I showed him. All of a sudden the convoy started exiting the forest and we hadn't started recording.

Everyone was shouting STOP STOP he said the flash of the headlights was to queue the convoy.

It took another hour and a half to regroup the convoy back in the woodlands.

Cosford

Now here we have one. Cameraman **John Randall** and I played in a band in the very early seventies (and still do). I had some pictures of John with permed hair from the mid 70s so I photocopied them to 400% and plastered them all over the walls at work for a laugh.

The following week JR and myself and a big crew had a really big OB location up in Cosford.

Charly Lowndes was the director. Production had booked the hotel. I travelled up with camera assistant **Mark Gosling** and checked in early, around 3 pm. I got room 16 and Mark got room

15. We met up at 7 pm for dinner. JR came in with a long face but wouldn't say what was up.

After a few drinks the beans were spilled and I found out what happened.

Because I put the pictures of JR up at work he thought he'd get his own back by phoning the hotel at lunchtime and telling them (pretending to be me) I had a bladder problem, and so they organised rubber sheets for my room: 17.

This is the funny bit. I was originally booked into room 17, but when I arrived it was a different person on reception, so when JR arrived two hours later he ended up getting room 17.

In other words, the rubber sheets were in JR's room. On arriving back at base a week later it seemed everyone knew what JR had planned except me. But I had the last laugh.

Scragtag the cat

Lots of adventures with Bluebird Productions, which was run by the late **Marcus Kimber** and **John Simons**.

We were filming in Chalfont St Giles and my car was parked in the Merlin's Cave pub car park. On returning to my car I saw a note in the window. It read, "Sorry about the dent - had to dash- here's my phone number".

I got back to base and **Gina Clark** (she was the p.a for the shoot) asked me if I was all right as I was thinking about the note.
I told her the story and she said "Phone him - he could be a millionaire and get you a new car."

I thought hard and I know my old Audi had lots of dents in it. Why not? So, retrieving the piece of paper, I made the call to a Mr M Phillips. The phone rang and I asked for Mr Phillips and the woman was very annoyed. Apparently I'd phoned Buckingham Palace.

We were filming with Director John Simons, for some kind of dinner do. It was an all-day thingy, so we set up in the morning, I hard wired a microphone to the lectern and being professional I gaffered the cables out of the way. The speaker came in the room and everyone was clapping. He walked straight past the lectern. Needless to say we couldn't hear a bloody thing.

We had an hour and a half to kill so we went to the bar. Three pints later we headed back to the 200 odd guests who had just finished their dessert.

With fish pole in hand I started booming their chat but then after fifteen minuets or so realised I needed the loo, but I didn't have any time to go, so muscle control came into play. Then all of a sudden muscle control gave way for a split second.

I looked down and my light thorn-coloured trousers now had the biggest wet patch you could imagine. The look on people's faces! Picture this: they are seated, I am standing with my arms in the air, displaying my groin area to all.

Weapons of Mass Detection

After three weeks filming a drama involving eight AK47 deactivated weapons, seven were returned to the hire company leaving one for the last day's shooting. **Bill Brackley** (our grips, driver) and I returned to barracks to finish off the last day's filming.

Queuing at the guard house at Blandford camp, we were collecting our passes when I noticed a Ghurkha waving his SA80 about and looking very troubled. Forgetting about the last AK47 on display in the back of our Range Rover, I ran outside to comfort the soldier.

So I opened the rear door to retrieve the weapon and proceeded to cock it. having a firearms certificate myself I adequately demonstrated safety catch procedure, cleared breech and so on to the Ghurkha

I was only trying to show him it was a deactivated gun, but Bill said afterwards I was lucky I didn't get a 5.62mm bullet in me.

I felt so sorry for this lovely guy who was only doing his job.

More downtime on a Blandford camp shoot, we all had a go on the rifle range. After doing my bit and not doing that well I decided to stand in the wings with my Olympus OM10 and snap a few pics of **Jon Poynter** and **Charlie Deane** shooting their Browning high power pistols.

Seconds later I felt a sharp pain in my left arm and dropped my camera. I'd only been shot by a 9mm round that had ricocheted off the sand pit debris and hit me.I still have the distorted bullet. And distorted arm lol.

One dub I remember doing involved a crew going to a drugs testing place in Farnborough. Top Gear **Chris Goffey** was presenting to camera, explaining how harmful certain drugs can be. But before he arrived we had to set up the camera and lights in this long room full of seized drugs.

There were plants everywhere, white powder stashes all over the place. Anyway, I was leaning on a table talking to the cameraman when I noticed all this white chalky stuff imbedded in my arm. Never been the same since.

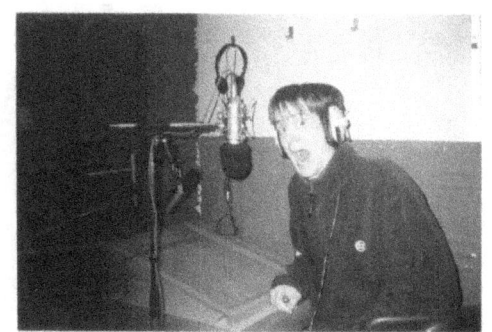

Dave Chapman

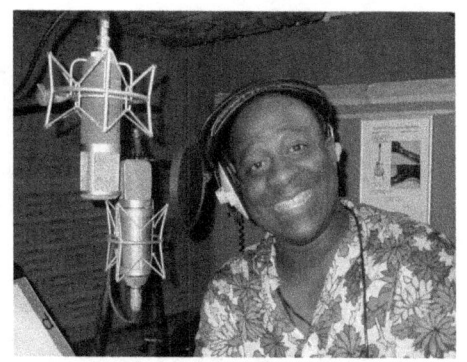

Dave Benson Phillips

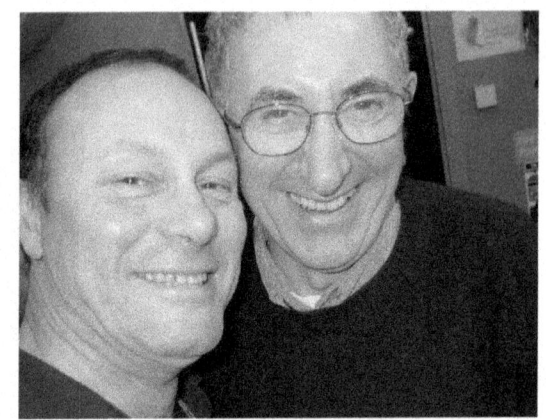

Fred Harris

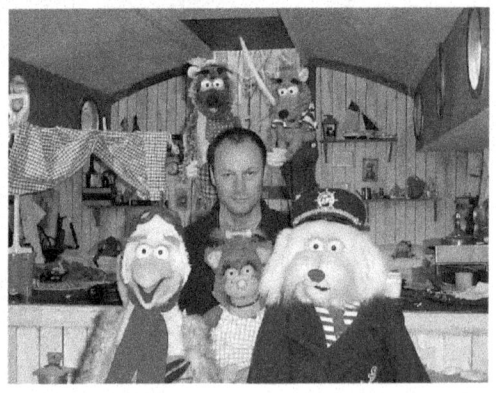

Beachcomber Bay

Porton down, Wiltshire

Filming a NBC (nuclear, biological and
chemical) training video at this highly secure site,
Jack McKenzie was the actor/presenter.

I was getting a lot of problems in the lab because
of fridge noises motors and all sorts ,
I wanted to get Jacks voice clean.

Asking if I could turn off the fridge I was told
NO! Then after pleading with "the scientists"
they said only for half an hour,' the cells within
would cultivate if let too long switched off' so I
turned it off and all sound was good.
Now when you turn off a noise source it makes
other masked sounds appear louder.
So I turned off another two fridges, recorded
jacks bit and that was that.

Anyway lunch time came and we headed off
down the pub, 2 hours later on returning I
realised the fridges were still switched off, shit!! I
turned them back on and said nothing.

Condoms

Going into town with (unit manager) **Cormack Clark** to buy 100 condoms less teats was embarrassing. We spent a day showing how cold weather can affect your blood cells.

We had a very large fish tank and had some bits of plastic representing ice and the red dye to represent blood. All we needed now was some teat less condoms to put all this in to look like blood cells, we could then immerse them in the fish tank of water and Bob's your uncle.

Because there wasn't any sound needed for this animated sequence, I volunteered going into town with Cormack Clark to find a Boots chemist.

So we queue up and as the lady said "How can I help you?" Cormack said "Have you got 100 teat less condoms?" looking at her face and then at all the people behind us in the queue thinking, here are two guys asking for a huge amount of johnnies.

I had to run out red-faced.

Another funny story, but not at the time, was working in Gosport with **Tim Hore** (cameras) at the Submarine Escape Training Tank, a deep filled tank where people learn to hold their breath from around 150 meters down and slowly exhale on the way up, to stop their lungs exploding. To record the sound I placed a Sony ECM77 inside a condom and weighted it so it dropped down the tank. Job done, sounded brilliant.

Got home to the wife five days later who found a handful of condoms in my suitcase. Nice one, Tim.

A production company called **Outsell** run by **Eddy Orr** was a nice little number if you like cars. Outsell had a contract with Honda so the filming for his company got us to all the motor shows: Geneva, London Earls Court and racing tracks in Italy.

Doing an interview with Formula1 legend **Damon Hill** was funny. As you may know, he's a guitarist as well . We finished the interview and then Eddy said to Damon "JR and Clint are in a band". Damon reached into his pocket and retrieved a plectrum. He thought that was pretty cool. I reached into my pocket and pulled out a bottle neck. You should have seen his face.

(That's a piece of copper piping you place on your finger to play slide guitar!)

Prime Minister Mrs Thatcher

An elite team from the television crew were
called upon to record **Mrs Thatcher**. In the 80s.
This was a five-minute piece to camera using
portaprompt.

This all went well until the lovely prime minister
asked if she could see and hear it back.
Well I had brought everything: two recorders,
two personnel mics and the kitchen sink, but no
speakers, and the office in No10 was a few floors
up, so to bring a Spendor BC1 in would have
been a nightmare, especially for a three-man
crew.

She kindly asked "Can I hear it back?" Oh shit,
but thinking very quickly I gave her my
headphones - bit greasy and being of the Beyer
dt100 sort they had crumbling black bits.
You know, the worn out ear muff look. She
looked at them and quickly decided to don them
upside down and not to spoil her perfect hair.

Things went very well for about a minute when
she said "I can't hear anything out of my right
ear." The headphone cable was stretched so hard
it had broken off the right leg wire in the jack
plug.

As Victor Meldrew would say, "God".

No soldering iron (if I had there wouldn't have been time for it to have warmed up). Decided to unscrew the jack cover and, with an enormous amount of pressure, hold the wire on to the jack plug with my thumb, thinking if the contact breaks she will look at me and repeat" I can't hear out my right ear". Five minutes seemed like eternity. I had an indentation in my thumb for two days.

Prime Minister Tony Blair

One of Eddy's jobs was at a motor show where **Tony Blair** and his missus were to attend. **Mark Gosling** managed to hit **Cherie Blair** in the head with his Anton Bauer battery. There was a planned route and I was to have my boom at the ready. My plan was to walk alongside Tony.

Mr Blair decided to take his own route and before I knew it he was heading towards me walking very fast. I turned and slipped. I was lucky I didn't fall completely over. As I slipped around 50 photographers flashed away. Somewhere someone's got a great pic of Tony with me in the background doing the hokey cokey.

Whitehall, London

Another funny one, but not funny at the time. We were called to Whitehall to record a piece to camera. I had two bvw50 video recorders in the van and decided once set up and working to use just one. I left the other one in the van.

Minutes before the Secretary of Defence **Tom** arrived I decided to record some bars and tone. This went well so I continued to sit around. At around a minute to go the warning light came on the machine and that was that.

The studio door opened, the Defence Secretary came in sat in front of the camera and his aide stood behind me just as I was unscrewing the lid on the machine to sort out the problem.

I pulled out the mangled tape , cut it with a pair of scissors, hoping that would release it, but to no avail then professionally replaced the lid and in a most embarrassed voice shouted "recording". That aide didn't know what to think. After a tear or so, rigger **Ross Cogswell,** who sat with me, laughed and said I was really studying the meters and fine tweaking levels. Luckily (and I did tell the Director) they didn't use the footage, as it was rubbish. Sorry, Tom.

The Queen

Buckingham Palace was my next port of call. I think it was around late 1992 as the piece was related to the First Gulf War for a video produced by Castle Productions...

Being assigned for the job in hand our first challenge was, "What do we call her?"
Marm was wrong - it was a military word. Then I was told Mum. I thought I couldn't call the queen Mum.

Then the powers to be said "How about Your Majesty?" I thought ok, I'd go for that one.

The day came. The elite force drove to London and through the side gates.

We were at Buckingham Palace, hooray! Got the kit up a few floors, set up and then we had tea and cucumber sandwiches all ready to go and **Ann C** (the director) announces "Your Majesty, let me introduce you to our crew." First **Jon** on cameras, then it was going to be me and as I stepped forward, lighting director **John F** stepped forward and trod on my foot.

Sorry, no pics.

I wasn't allowed to put a personal mic on Her Majesty so I rigged up two Sennheiser 416s aimed at her on the left side. Obviously one was backup, but Lizzy did give me a worried look as the mics did look even to me like two rocket launchers

I don't think the Queen forgave me as a few months later we were at RAF Marham and I was told not to use my pole (that is a pole with a microphone on it) as Her Majesty didn't want people to know what she was saying.

Well, while all the crews at the air show were fannying about I thought, just go for it, extended to about 10 foot, in goes the mic, If looks could kill." To the tower!"echoed in my head
I just thought it's got to sound better than not to have it at all.

Going back to the palace it was a wrap and we were getting the gear out the side gate. A footman with I think five corgis was about to take the dogs on a walk around the grounds,

It had to be done. Now listen, I love dogs. I have two of my own, but I had to do it. I lightly, carefully kicked one of the corgis up the arse.

NOT hard, I repeat not hard. How many soundmen can say they did that? Those doggie eyes said it all.

More Royalty shenanigans

Derrick Cunningham was directing, **Nigel Williams** cameraman the scene was at an airfield the program was 'low level instrument landing', I know, it sounds boring but it was far from that.

Flying in an Andover prop aircraft at 100ft then 1000ft then 100ft is quite daunting.

Luckily whilst on board I just had to record the chatter from the cockpit on my nagra reel to reel. We all felt very sick.

The next day was a lovely day, it was mid summer and very hot, we had to shoot some exteriors, so it was going to be on the airfield of the Andover up and pass 1000ft to 100ft and so on.

We parked the van around 100 yards from the runway and walked to the tarmac and plonked ourselves down.

We could see the Andover circling about a mile away this went on for about forty-five minutes.

So I decided to strip off and enjoy the sun ,
twenty minutes or so later a RAF land rover came
screeching up to us and a Lovely Corporal
shouted 'put your shirt back on' apparently Fergy
wouldn't take off while I was laying next to the
runway half naked

Another **Ann C** funny one was a programme on
the BFPO (British Forces Post Office), this little
number that got us filming all over the World:
Bangkok, Saudi, Germany and, oh yeah,
Caversham, yes the one near Reading, Berks.

I remember doing a POV of a parcel going round
on a conveyer belt (oh, that's what a parcel sees!)
We must have looked like a right load of berks.

In Caversham we had this cul-de-sac where we
planted a fake letterbox. Do I have to explain
why? Okay, yes. If we had to do a retake then we
would have had to phone up the Royal Mail.

Quicker to have your own letterbox and just lift it
up and get your letter out the bottom and redo the
take. We had some strange looks from the
residents though.

Enter postman. We wanted to show all the
hazards of a postman's life, so a dog was put into
the equation Trouble is dog didn't want to know.
Dog was more interested in my furry mic cover

than postman. I was booming overhead but the dog just wouldn't have it.

I ended up taking off the Rycote windjammer and sticking it in the postman's bag.
We had some good takes but the dog sussed out where the windjammer was hidden and proceeded to rip the postman's bag and jacket to shreds.

With SSVC we did all the Forces training films, from tanks, planes to M3s. M3s you ask? We'll talk about this amazing amphibious vehicle later. Anyway..

One of the training programmes was about the SA80. Second day filming we watched these guys running towards us, falling down and half the plastic furniture of the rifles fell off.

Later, after a lot of hanging around, got the urge to have a wee. Off I went to a quiet part of the forest and had a wee. Seconds later a cammed up soldier stood up and yells at me to fuck off!!! Shit, I'd weed on him. Sorry mate.

Who found this location: motorway, dog kennels, saw mill and aeroplanes? Asking actor **Jack Mackenzie** to memorise three sheets of A4. He was so professional, but we had this giggling thing where I had to turn my back and laugh, then he had to go all the back to the beginning. Who picks these locations?

Legoland, Denmark

We did a promotion video in Denmark; I think it was a three-day shoot, in Legoland, We all had Lego land hats given to us so we wrote our names in pen on the front of them. **Russell Hearne** had Russ, **Mark Hearn** had Mark, Sharron had Sharron and I had Clint.

Little did I know some sad life had changed my CLINT to - you guessed it - joined the the L and the I together. What a complete twat for not realising that.
Spent the next two days wearing it.

I had a laugh with Tim though at Euro Disney, Paris, Sharron Hollins and I waited inside the amusement park for Tim to return from the car park with some Anton bauer batteries.

I left it around fifteen minutes and speaking into the walkie talkie said in a Jamaican accent "Hello there, where are you, boy?" Little did I know Tim was just coming back into the park and the Jamaican guy was checking the stamp on his hand, everyone could hear my voice. Sorry Tim!

Tony Fewkes Airbus

We did a week's shoot at the Airbus factory then the following week the crew, Tim Hoare and myself had to film from a vehicle carrying the airbus wing down the motorway. This was going to be cool, as sound and VO were going to be added later so I was free to be the driver.

A police Range Rover was our escort, so imagine this artic lorry with a fucking great plane wing on the back, and a police car escorting it. I was driving in and out and undertaking and overtaking and slowing down and accelerating pass the police car once again.
 I was in heaven.I don't think anyone else in the world could say they'd done that!!

Swallow Hotel York

This Army job involved nothing to do with what happened at the weekend. Staff kindly asked us if we didn't mind one hundred and fifty deer hounds coming to the hotel. It was one of those convention thingies. We finished filming at the camp and on return to the hotel you wouldn't believe it, dogs everywhere.

Cameraman **Tim Hore** had a Mars bar in his jacket pocket; he went to his room, filled the basin up with warm water and left the chocolate bar to melt a bit.

After some clever reshaping and with a little quiff on the end he decided to place it in the hotel lift. The next morning all you could smell was bleach.

Anyway so much to write about Tim. It will have to be in book two!

BFBS Radio

BFBS was situated in the heart of Paddington, London. Yes, as in Paddington Bear.
We had several trips up to the West End.
One evening I was in the Black Bull pub, In South Ruislip and a black cab friend of mine had sculptured a wooden picture of Cliff Richard.

I said to him, I'm seeing Cliff at the BFBS studios next week, he said, "Can you get it autographed for me?" I said I'll give it a try.

Now my song-writing partner and I had written this song called "Don't Leave Me Now" and I had it on cassette (old format).
We thought Cliff could sing this number and an opportunity I really couldn't afford to miss. So, sitting there with my boom next to Cliff, recorded

the interview. Filming was finished. I hesitated and said "Cliff, err, err, er … will you sign this carving?"Wrong move. He signed it and left. I still have the cassette.

Director **Chris Wilson** was involved in the next BFBS Radio, TV shoot. It was with **Uri Gellar,** He managed to re-start some watches and clocks in the Falklands.Same situation: we were all sat around a DJ's studio. **Tommy Vance** was the interviewer. Even though Tommy was doing the interview Uri kept taking his eye line away from him and looking me in the eyes. Anyway, said goodbye.

Entered the BFBS lift with JR and the microphone just fell off of the boom;; the 3/8 thread had just snapped in half Not thinking too much about this incident, we loaded the van, and we were now waiting for Director Chris Wilson to return.

And he did, with a half bent spoon. We drove down the A40 West Way and Chris held this spoon in front of me and to my amazment I could still see it bending. Very dangerous as I was driving.

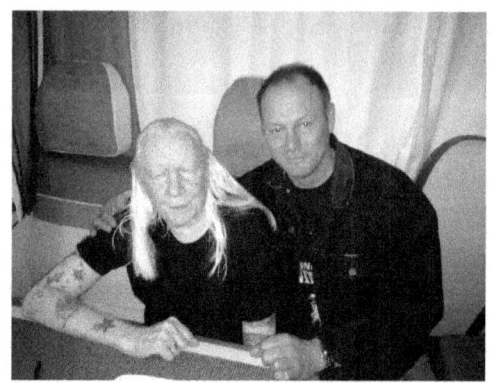

Johnny Winter

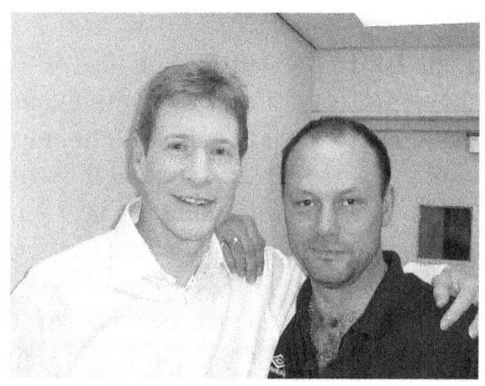

Paul Jones

Toy fair Harrogate

We had done this gig for a few years now. We'd
drive up to Haringey, do a recce, go to hotel,
drink, meet press people, job done. I think this
was the third year, with **Russell Hearne**
presenting.

It was a lovely B&B we stayed in , an oldy woldy
with a beautiful matchstick model of a boat
sitting on top of the fire place. Long story cut
short, I tripped, knocked the boat off the fire
place, but – worse - trod on it. I apologised and
went to bed.

Next morning didn't feel that great, but got
through the day, forgetting about the night before
packed up my sound kit ready to go home. We
loaded up the van and went back to the press
office for a cuppa, then I heard a walkie talkie. It
was a biker cop, He came in and said "Is there a
Clint Nurse here?" Well I was froze, or should I
say I shit myself?

He arrested me, handcuffed and cautioned me
about some criminal damage in a B&B put me in
a room and said because he was a bike cop I
would have to wait 15 minutes for the van to take
me to the Police station.

After what seemed like a hell of a wait, all the
press office PR people arrived with their cameras

and took a picture of me. I was not impressed – it was a big wind up!

In the end the good cop felt sorry for me and escorted us from the exhibition to the motorway (with blue flashing light) - that felt good.

Working in Germany with Producer/Director **Jonathan Marks** was great. Being a soundman himself he helped me on my way. Finishing at five thirty and heading back to the hotel, by going slowly we could add another 15 minutes to our time sheets. When we arrived late at the hotel Jonathan said "Why has it taken so long?" I said "The van only does 60 miles an hour." This worked for a few days, then he said "I don't believe you." He opened the speedo assembly and removed the tachograph which read the van had done 90 miles an hour.

Helicopters

Sound recording in aircraft can be difficult. In the early years I would stick an ECM 55 small condenser mic into the headset.

This worked quite well until the Army Air Corp gave me a NATO jack plug It's a plug with around five contacts that only work in aircraft. They said you can take pins I and 2 as ears and 3 and 4 as mics, (I can't remember for certain.) Anyway, this worked brilliantly: nice clean audio. And it worked on many shoots.

Now, no-one told me there are two types of NATO jacks: short ones, long ones and two ways of wiring them. Everything was good for I think a year or two. I was very proud to have "my own NATO jacks" which worked on Hercules C120s until a Falklands visit, We were just about to take off in a Gazelle helicopter . I plugged in my NATO jack and BANG! blew all the communication fuses.

Some of the best and worst experiences have been with helicopters. Not being told at 1,000 feet that we were about to do an emergency landing. I think my pants made their own way to the hotel cleaners.

But one of the best flights was in Kowloon, Hong Kong. A little Scout helicopter: pilot on the right, cameraman Jon Pointer on the left and me in the back, doors off, feet on skids and letting the cameraman actually control the bvw50 using the umbilical cord, which allowed me to click away on my Olympus OM10 SLR, and get some very impressive aerial shots.But saying that, I had no communication and as we were hovering over Kowloon airport to my right and upwards I saw a jumbo 747 heading towards us.

I daren't tap the pilot on the shoulder, and I couldn't speak to anyone, so I managed to alert the pilot by, yes, finally tapping him on the shoulder. I thought, if I distract him and we crash it would be a quicker death than a 747 flying through us. He descended rapidly.

Some things that have made my day

Being allowed in the hall first to mic up the lectern for Prime Minister **John Major** and a BBC soundman who'd arrived later asks for a feed from my mixer, No problem BBC man, he was very happy so I said here's my card! Hoping to get some work for the future.

Bastard never called!

A weeks filming in Salisbury Plain, we were wet, tired and it was raining. We were all heading back to the Hotel when I noticed **Mark Hearn** in the lighting van , I looked in my rear view mirror to see Mark had put his windscreen washers on, I was pissing myself, I had filled his washer bottle with chocolate powder. He arrived at the hotel much later.

Waking up at the Crown Hotel in Salisbury, opening the curtains and watching the reactions of around 20 people on the upstairs of a bus staring at me literally 20 feet away. I was naked and the window was at hip level.

Waking up one morning in Germany at 7.00am for breakfast. I banged on all the crews hotel doors and headed to the dining room. No one there, so I asked the cleaner in my broken German: "Ensholdegon ze bitte [excuse me please] vat time iz brekfazt [what time is breakfast]?" She just looked at me and said in English "The clocks went back last night and the time is 6 oclock."We have all now got to sit around in our rooms for an extra hour…

I won't mention the time JR managed to get CS gas on his todger ,next book I think.
No..Ive changed my mind.

CS Gas joke

On returning from Germany with some CS gas blanks for our blank firing guns, JR noticed my blanks had green fungi on them.

So I wrapped them in cling film to stop them getting contact with our skin.

Weeks later we did an Abbey National shoot in studio two we showed everyone the blanks .
Lunch time we managed to get a session down the pub with the crew.
Once back we rehearsed the shots, had a wee break, JR returned screaming, he had only touched the CS leaking blanks and then held his old chap, we all fell about laughing.

Pulling a prank with Producer Sharron (scared of spiders) Hollins. Picture this: live Television, opening titles, I put a fake spider under her script, cut to studio Sharron picks up her script …
SCREAM!! We lost the first pictures of our presenter. Sorry, Sharron.

On this location **Jon** was annoying squaddies as he did. As the guys were putting their cam cream on , we decided to smear some around his view finder. And as Jon put his eye to the rubber he obviously felt the cream but chose to ignore it out of stubbornness.

When he took his eye away from the view finder had a black ring around his eye, turning him into Panda Man. Jon pretended nothing was untoward and looked an idiot for half an hour or so.

Funny Moments

Live studio broadcast ,Sitting at the sound mixing desk , **Rory O'sullivan** by my side on vision mixer when all of a sudden a roll of gaffer tape tumbled down , I saw this in slow motion , It was heading towards the vision mixer , Rory just calmly caught it and calmly carried on.

Walking two feet away from hundreds of landmines and anti-personnel mines on the Falkland sands and then five minutes later cutting my hand on my Leatherman.

Falklands, 1984, weeing on an electric fence and not getting electrocuted. I think there is a scientific reason for this, all to do with the gaps in the wee flow or something. to much information.

If a presenter forgets their earpiece, I have a box in the sound control room with a very very large ear piece and some marmite pressed into the hole simulating ear wax and a solitary pubic hair attached. (Not really a pube).

They don't forget next time.

Studio 2 and Animals

I vaguely remember a job in Studio 2 involving monkeys and exotic birds and a Giant viper. This guy was presenting to, I think, a three-camera studio production. I preferred to boom this guy as animals were crawling all over him and I didn't want any mics to be eaten. The studio floor was in a right state, animal cages, clothes, cables and all sorts and I had to find a place to stand to boom our presenter.

After the monkey piece came the snake, a twenty-foot viper. Anyway, next up was a parrot, so I took my stance over a massive blanket, boom extended fully and all sounded well. Ten minutes later I recomposed myself only to realise I was straddling a giant viper between my legs. Good talking point down the pub.

On my first actual job assisting JR in lighting, at Sandhurst, John erected an HMI light with a wind-up stand and then locked it off, after filming he asked me to unwind the light. I can't remember what I did wrong but the whole HMI came down like thunder. For about five years JR made me feel bad about his HMI with a bent yoke.

I don't think I hit it off with JR for the first two months. Week two my mum made me cheese sandwiches; I know - I was 32 years old.

The 2k blond lights had a grill in front of the bulb to stop glass shattering everywhere, I thought this was a good platform for my cheese toasty, until the cheese melted all over the lamp.

I was not popular. This was a sight, JR on camera in a cherry picker 100 feet above the crew filming an exercise on the Brüggen airfield for two hours; we had an hour and a half break in some German hotel bar, after a session in a bar.

We returned to the airfield. JR went back up in the cherry picker and we were left under him. We must have had three or four wees before realising that he hadn't had any, how he didn't wee on us. I don't know, but I'm so glad.

My love of guns led me to taking my weapons to military establishments. Speaking to Inspector Edwards of Ruislip police station gave me all the peace of mind on taking them on location with me.
That was until one morning, when we were driving to a Royal Navy base in Plymouth and my gun was in my hand luggage. Normally we

would check in at the hotel beforehand and with police approval would have the gun put in a safe.

When we arrived at the navy base: it was on **Amber alert**. "Excuse me, sir; can I check your bags?"
I'm thinking, shit I've got a 357 magnum revolver in my hand luggage with rounds.

He put his head to each bag and prodded and poked around all of them and then said "Open this one". Jon's case was opened. What a relief. Never again.

Salisbury Plain

I remember filming late at night and we were waiting ages for something to happen, so we put some empty coke cans in a tree and started firing .22 rounds from a Smith & Wesson Chief Special revolver. My wife's Uncle Dick lent it to me, shooting at night is very hard and we didn't realise we were missing the cans. The rounds were heading towards Boscombe Down, around two miles away and near the very expensive Tornados.

Clouds of the World

Great idea I had on location one time.
If you are trying to do a low shot (baby legs)
looking up at a building, fine until the guy from
the adjacent building comes over complaining
that you are filming his building.
You say your building is not in the shot but they
insist on watching the rushes back or even getting
very aggressive and asking us to move on.

I've invented a time code cue sheet called *clouds
of the world*; you pretend your filming clouds not
your annoying persons building.
If they ask to see the tape back you just say fuck
off its nothing to do with you.

Puppets

During the 2000s I seemed to get to record entire
puppet shows.
I loved it … Beachcomber Bay, three series,
something special with **Justin Fletcher**, **Mr
Tumble**, four series, and working with Big Dave,
Dave Benson Phillips, on PJ's Bedtime on the
Disney Channel series in 2003 and loads more.

Matt Greenwood was VT operator for
Beachcomber Bay, This was a thirteen week
shoot in all, so a few laughs were in order. I
recorded the Director saying " run to record "

Now I could see the VT return feed in the sound control room, so it made the day go really fast when every time I played "run to record" down to VT I would see the time code running in record mode. Sorry Matt.

Bubble and Squeak for Nickelodeon and so the puppets go on. I must admit I had such a laugh working on these productions I learnt a lot about puppeteers' techniques.

Chatterbox productions

This production was another puppet type show. It involved a couple of presenters and an invisible character.

In the wings was the great Roy Skelton doing the voice over's for our invisible character.

I had to 'play in' some pre-recorded voices onto the studio floor speaker from an old sonifex cart machine; these machines were popular with radio DJs, but the problem with these units they took a very long time to re-cue.

So the only alternative I had was using a reel to reel with a load of coloured leader tape and a lot of concentration. With the start and stopping of the tape we got there in the end.

As well as providing the iconic *Rainbow* voices, Roy Skelton also voiced several *Doctor Who* villains including the Daleks, Roy told me he would sit in the wings and with the aid of a controller operates the Dalek lights with his voice activated microphone. He also did the voices for the Cybermen and the Krotons

[3].

Roy William Skelton (20 July 1931 – 8 June 2011) television for nearly fifty years, most notably the characters of both Zippy and George on Rainbow, which the actor first joined in the early 1970s and performed on until it was axed in 1992.

Roy was a lovely person.

Easy life

Easiest shoot in the world: met at Harwich docks, then sailed to Holland, few drinks on ship, get picked up, and travel to Sennelarger, Germany, many hours later.

We stayed in a hotel, and in the morning, travelled to the firing ranges, we kept the camera in the van and sat and waited at the SA80 rifle 300m range to pick up three or four shots (excuse the pun).

It rained for hours, didn't even get the kit out.

Travelled back the next day, more drinks on the ship, arrive home, thank you, **Roger Coy** (Producer Director).

Some of the productions we have done in Studio 2 and 3 at Chalfont Grove have been memorable. **X certificate**, a Channel 5 late night soft porn channel was recorded in Studio 2.

It was basically two settees, two presenters and some porn stars and playing video clips. **Ben Dover**, and **Neil Down** and a guy with a 12-inch dick were there with some girl with ridiculous size boobs, 55DDD or something.

She had trouble on the plane from America despite having a valve under her arm to reduce her breasts.

When she arrived at the studio I think she overdid the pumping up. I walked into the studio and saw a young lady bending - BEN DOVER get it? - over.

I thought, cute arse then realised she had no head. On close inspection I realised she had bent over and with her humungous boobs couldn't get back up again. Being a perfect gent, I.................................walked off.

Fat Academy

Studio 2 pre-recorded this series for channel 4 all about keeping fit and fat people losing weight.

Ex TV Breakfast show presenter **Penny Smith** presented this one; she's a really funny person and is great to work with. I'd have four fat people brought to the sound control for miking. As always I would say "Do you need the toilet first?" and no was normally the answer.

On two episodes I had a women come back to me looking very sheepish and giving me my transmitters packs which have been down the pan.
All the hassle of borrowing a microphone or two from other studios, and changing channels etc and above all sending the pack back to Audio Limited for repair and costing loads of money.

National Army Museum, London

SPOTY (**S**ports **P**ersonality **O**f **T**he **Y**ear) award.
Every year we filmed this event. I remember
JR's lighting very well. He put up a polecat (an
adjustable pole with suckers on each end and you
fix it across large alcoves).

John attached a 2000w lamp (blonde) to this pole
to light up a wall of very large paintings which
were probably a couple of hundred years old.
Half hour or so later I noticed a scorch mark on
this painting that had to be at least 15' x 6' in
size.
That's still a secret to this day! Owwps !!

Peter always had the best job of sitting in the OB
truck while muggins had to grin and bare the
freezing January winds doing the boom swinging,
only wearing a suit. Brrrrr

Sandhurst

After filming on a wooded training area in
Sandhurst, we headed back to base. Just then I

noticed a yellow ammo box sitting by a tree. In actual fact I saw loads. **Tim Hoare** had one of these as a toolbox, which I thought was cool so anyway I put the yellow ammo box in the van.

Several hours passed and an Army Major called to see if anyone had seen a yellow ammo box as a squaddie was still in the woods looking for his landmark. I owned up, got a bollocking and gave it back.

Travelling back to base in the rain was quite funny . The camera platform/sun roof used to leak. Charlie Deane and I had to wear waterproof hoodies because every time we braked a gallon of water would pour on to our heads.

Wearing hoodies whilst driving was hilarious, every time I turned to speak to Charlie the hood would still face forward and vice versa, so we couldn't see each other.

Studio 3 with Land Rover

Rob Lewin was the star here. He was technical coordinator. We did live broadcasts to car dealerships all over the country; this one was for

Land Rover, and it featured good friend **Julie Peasgood** plus four guests.

All radio mic'd with some spare hardwired ecm77 microphone around the back. All going well for 30 odd minutes then radio mic 4 went down. I had backups on the desk but they had put all their scripts over them. (I told them not to.)

Rob didn't say a word, but quietly crept onto the studio floor. Now I'm thinking, what's he doing and where is he? Then a hand appeared from it looked like between the legs of guest number two, the one whose mic wasn't working, and he clipped the backup mic on.

What a pro!

Rob appeared again as my aide on this three-day studio broadcast. This one was a Xerox telethon: five languages, five booths, full virtual studio (that's blue or green screen chroma key if you didn't know).

I was running low on groups sending out the different languages, and normally it was only four languages which would have been fine as the desk only has four groups.

So I used a send that went through an FX processor. Yep, it was on bypass so the effect in question wasn't heard.

It was around an hour and a quarter later, I got a complaint about the Portuguese translation, realising the FX processor was on "wet", meaning the Portuguese translation was going through the effect. The effect was on Pitch minus. Shit, the commentator sounded like Barry White.

The second day was a disaster; my doctor gave me some pills which reacted with the pill I was on already on and that was that. Good old Rob.

I'm mixing 20 faders, Rob on my right with the sick bucket. Literally every 30 seconds, there I go again. Because my sound control door is always open I could see the reflection of a studio tour in my monitor.

On the break I lay down on the sound dubbing couch felt like shit and was taken home after two hours.

Thailand, Puckett

Thailand again, this time with a telecommunications company. It was a fly on the wall type follow the staff around 24 hours a day.

We were filming their meetings, lunch breaks and in the evening watching the "lady men" entertain.

On arriving at the airport I had to ask a customs official to confirm my curiosity is it pooket,fooket,fuket

He just looked at me in that 'we execute foreigners 'look. I thought Foock It.

I would come out of my room to go to breakfast at 7.30 in the morning and as you open the door the heat from the sun was around 20 degrees and all the lizards condescend around the door, so it's a quick exit so the little critters don't get into to your room.

Seven days later job done, the director's treat was a trip around the market oh and by the way sure I saw a dead body around the back of the veg barrow. Then an elephant's trek.

This sounded so cool; we had two of the crew on the front elephant and three of us on the rear one. All went well until the boy on our elephant started stabbing the poor thing on head with a 'snow type pick' the elephant in front pissed all over our elephant when I say pissed I mean (fireman hosed) us.

I remember our elephant's feet on the edge of a cliff; I thought if he falls we are dead. We were about a thousand feet up.

Any way on the way back down our elephant decided to stop under a weird looking tree and on close inspection above my head was a gigantic ants nest, they were entering and exerting a giant green cocoon, so I had words with elephant and 'snow type pick' rider and reluctantly plodded on.

Great shoot

Hong Kong

This was the last year before retirement for our boss **Peter Jenkins**. He wanted to come on location with us. The only trouble was we were all scared of him, especially me, as in the early days Peter Jenkins - sorry Mr Jenkins - was walking through VT with Producer Barry Warden and as I passed in the opposite direction said out loud "Hi Barry, hello Jenkins!"

So his stay in Hong Kong was a little uneasy, unloading the van one day I pulled the fish pole out of the van and managed to land it neatly in Mr Jenkins's chest, leaving him gasping for air.

I think at the end of the day he forgave me as I wrote a song called farewell JPJ (John Peter Jenkins) and all of the production staff sang it, using sound dubbing to its extreme and later mimed in the pop video.

I also remember doing this trick at Sand Hurst. We were filming in a small officer's room and I was booming the mike. As I reversed I managed to smash a 100 year old document on the wall behind me. You should have seen there faces.

Temple Street, Hong Kong, 1985

You are supposed to pay $200 to film in Temple Street, Kowloon, and Hong Kong Island...Unless your name is **Chris** (Producer/Director). What a fantastic street: snake charmers and loads of stuff.... Oh, and some woman sitting in the gutter, peeling a frog, alive too.

Jon. Cameraman was told by Chris to hold the camera facing backwards so the authorities wouldn't suss out what we were doing, so I held the boom backwards (well I've done this before in the early years), but the Chinese sussed it and it got quite hairy to say the least.

They chased us with weapons. We rushed into a multi-storey car park and waited. And waited. Chris looked down over the side. I said "Keep back!" Too late, they saw us and we ran like fuck down the back stairway and got away, never to return. …should have paid the $200 Chris.

Scotland

Edinburgh was another hairy place. You're right, the jocks are hairy. Boom boom.
Radio DJ **Mark** from Middlesborough joined our team to film in Scotland,

Mark, director **Richard Barnes,** the PA, hangers-on, all of them went off to recce the next location leaving moi and JR (**John Randall)** to stand in the middle of Edinburgh square with all the kit.

We are talking about £200,000 of goodies. Now Edinburgh is not short of the odd tramp. Where is a policeman when you want one?

Mark, Richard Barnes and a crew went to Amsterdam for a two day shoot.

We stayed in the Hilton Hotel for just one night. It was amazing. phone in the bathroom etc.

We spent around an hour in the room and then met in reception we headed into the town. Before we knew it we were in the red light district. I remember seeing this guy bantering with a scantly clad woman in a window.

He put up five fingers. *Guess that meant five guilders.* And he went in. After our meal we walked back passed the same girl and just for a laugh did a five finger. She gave me a two finger. I don't understand.

I remember doing sound on Mark Page's pop spot. He had loads of guests like **Mandy Smith, Bill Wyman's** girlfriend, and **Sandy.** Now Sandy was my first love - you know schoolboy fantasy, short skirt, bare feet etc. (Bare feet, believe me, were trendy in the sixties). You sure I hear you ask!

Now I had her to myself, so nervously I tried to place a radio mic on her and ended up lightly touching her face. She heavily flinched and told me to get off. "You scratched my face!" ... Shit. Later I thought, stupid cow, trying to make a comeback at your age.

STATUS QUO

We shot a day's worth of trailers in a West London recording studio with Status Quo. **Francis Rossi** and **Rick Parfitt** were promoting their compilation CD for "Timelife", a shopping music channel.

We arrived early to set up. All was going well until cameraman Mark Gosling trapped his hand in the 'Merlin Arm' (a camera tracking device that can crane up and down). VERY HEAVY!

The famous duo turned up and we did several takes. Some giggling and memory loss was part of the morning's shenanigans.
Rick took an interest in my Fender Telecaster which I just happened to bring with me. Later they both signed it. Hehe.

During a break they disappeared, I had a sandwich, and then decided to play the studios grand piano and do some of my own stuff.

Five minutes or so later I felt a presence by my left ear. It was Francis whispering, "don't give up the day job".

Thanks mate….. I didn't .

Tympani Productions

Tim Hoare and **Penny King** run this very well managed company. I've been to America a lot with Tympani working with Xerox. Open night jamming was on Monday at the bar.

 Jez Shervell and **Sam Robinson** from Xerox would be there, along with the film crew, Tim, Penny and **Stuart Brown** , A great night out, Rochester NY is the place with the Dinosaur Bar blues jam and some well-known artists.

We did a shoot the next day in Rochester graveyard. I think it's one of the biggest; it's around a mile long.

It was a very cold week that week. There was all this snow in the ground and **Sam Robinson** had to do a 'long shot' piece to camera with me using a radio mic.
Because the snow was so deep Sam couldn't see where he was treading and also had to train his eyeline on the camera and proceeded to plough straight through a handful of graves. I swear to this day I saw a dark figure behind him.

In 2004 I sold my **Pete Townshend** Gibson SG at Christies on 27th September. Three days later we arrive in Rochester, New York with Xerox, did a morning's filming and then found a place for lunch. Opposite was a guitar shop.

I said I'm just going to pop across the road to see what they have got in the shop and, lo and behold, on the vintage wall was a white 1963 Gibson SG Special 400 serial numbers younger than the Pete SG I sold and in perfect nick.

So I bought it.

We did a Xerox shoot in Little Chalfont in Buckinghamshire, after filming I took the sound kit and camera back to the vehicle in the car park. As I was waiting for the crew to return I noticed a woman who couldn't lock her car. She had one of those remote controllers. I went to her rescue but to no avail.

She left the car open and went shopping, while she had gone I decided to rearrange the back of the car, and then I noticed the Script Boy, a device which transmits time code to a PA's (production assistant's) clipboard (do I have to explain everything?) was left on.

I then realised this lady's car was on the same frequency as the Script Boy, if my memory serves me well around 440MHZ.

So I couldn't help myself, when she returned I kept switching the Script Boy on and off and to my amusement watched this little old lady having trouble with her door locks.

Lewis Hamilton The McLaren factory, Langley

We were shown around the factory before Lewis Hamilton arrived. It would have been nice to check the kit first.

We arrive an hour later to the interview room, opened flight cases and, oh shit, forgot radio mic cables.
Lewis Bartley the cameraman walks in. I said to Lewis "Do you have anything?" He said "There's more kit in the car, which is three floors down." Take a left, take a right and shit I'm lost.

We got by.

I ended up radio miking Simeon and booming Lewis. Split tracks 1 and 2 and edited it in Adobe Audition for radio.

Ladysmith Black Mambazo at the Albert Hall

Being a muso, this was a privilege and pleasure for me. We were in the dressing room, they were waiting to go on stage. I managed to record some stunning harmonies with a single sennheiser 416 overhead and, with their unique technique, it sounded phenomenal. Really wish I had my compact flash recorder then.

Box Office Boys

Another production I have enjoyed doing is the *Box Office Boys* for BFBS TV. This production is all about a couple of funny guys previewing movies. And doing spoofs (if you guess the spoof, you win the DVDs).

I think we have to date done 105 episodes. **Paul Hendy** and **Richard Orford** were the presenters.

We've been all over the world with *Box Office Boys*: Kosovo, Germany, Cyprus RAF Halton and the Falklands (for nine hours). That one was good. We boarded a jumbo jet at Brize Norton. 100 people on board means one person to three seats. I remember taking my portable DVD player and watching Final Destination on it.

Every time something happened in the film our plane dropped or banked, I must have turned the film off around four times until I thought this is so unlucky. I put the DVD away.

We arrived at Ascension and refuelled, took off again (still three seats each). Arrived at Mount Pleasant and watched the Harry Potter film, had some red wine, slept four hours and then flew back.

We flew to Cyprus where Paul Hendy plays Ursula Andres from a James Bond movie. I can tell you now it wasn't pleasant watching Paul change in the truck.

Rabbits in Chalfont

SSVC/BFBS base is situated in a vast wooded area in Chalfont Grove, near Gerrards Cross, Buckinghamshire. The room 785 studios are situated in the studio 1 building but during the summertime we would set up an outside link to a shed in the grounds named 'The summer house' It was situated over in a wooded area. Now there are lots of rabbits and some deer on the grounds

Standing outside the summerhouse with boom and mic raised high and ready waiting for the action I suddenly fell down around a foot through a rabbit warren, blimey Richard Orford nearly

had a microphone stabbed into his temple.
Luckily no rabbit was hurt.
Heart rate now 120 bpm…Rabbits 600 bpm

Computers

Computers were Producer /Director **Charly Lowndes** greatest forte, but not this day.
Charly left his computer outside his office one night and before he knew it security called the bomb disposal unit and performed a controlled explosion, blowing Charlie's new pc to smithereens

BFN, British Forces News, with **Kate** presenting. Cameraman **Andy Rodger** dashed in a minute before going on air, saying "We can hear talkback on the floor".

I rushed onto the floor. I heard talkback really loud and placed my ear to Kate's back, ran my ear down her tube, and there it was; a split in the plastic bit connected to the diaphragm. Sounds like surgery!

Then I heard "Forty seconds!" really loud from PA **Laura Adams.** It was spilling from the severed gap.

I was calm and collected and shouted "Gaffer tape anyone?" **Andy Rodger** on cameras threw me a roll of camera tape. I very quickly taped up the split, ran back into the gallery. Kate said "That's louder" and talkback bleeding solved with 10 seconds to go.

A recent live interview on BFBS News, I can't remember who the guest was, but I put the radio mic on him and slipped the transmitter in his pocket.

Did the interview. He came back into the gallery and I pulled the transmitter very slowly by the cable out of his pocket and said "Cheers!"

Then I realised the clip on the back of the audio limited transmitter had picked up a wad of £20 notes from his pocket and as I held the radio pack the stash went neatly into the palm of my hands.

Instantly I realised this and returned his money. Three times this has happened to date.

National Lottery

We had a job in Studio 3. I think it was the Rugby with **Paul Hendy**, **Paul Bunks** and **Richard Orford**. We were told our sandwiches were in Studio 2's green room, sitting on the side, which by the way was the **National Lottery's** studio base. I couldn't find any food in the green room but noticed an M&S bag on the side. After throwing out a couple of bananas and a packet of crisps found a BLT sandwich (a triple mind you). I took it away and enjoyed it. Didn't realise all our sandwiches were in the fridge.

Minutes later got a right bollocking from the runner! I had eaten **Dale Winton**'s dinner.

During recording Euro Millions **Jon** (producer and sports presenter) asked for the numbers up-front for a joke so he could wind up his wife and read out the numbers as they are called and pretend to win, because we pre-recorded the show from Paris and relayed it an hour later, so the numbers had already been drawn. I phoned Jon with the numbers, who proceeded to convince his wife they had won £150 million.

… They are still married.

We had girl band on the National Lottery. Four of them were outside having a fag with no make-up on..Yes, Cheryl, you! Where was my camera when I needed it?

I walked passed and said "Hi Girls" ……They just looked at me. I felt such a prat.

On my Annual leave (one week) decorating the house I had a call at ten o'clock from Head engineer **Chris Cotton.** Apparently the freelance soundman hadn't turned up so Chris stepped in to help Sharron's Room 785 sound recordings. So whilst painting the skirting boards I mentally portrayed a picture of my mixer to Chris (who was in the studio) on which faders to push up.

He did fine, the freelancer turned up and that was that. Next morning and to this day I get a lot of flack that all my job entails is "one fader". Thanks Chris.

Howard Heyward

Underwater diving sound dub, this was my bag:. A totally mute training programme, apart from the commentary and, atmosphere needed.

Howard and I sat down and it just clicked between us. Big jar of water, two straws and as the divers released oxygen from their tanks we blew into the water, slowed it down (didn't have pitch shifters then), a bit of dark reverb - job done!

SSVC won a BAFTA award from this production

I'm thinking to myself this must be the end of an era, 32 years at Chalfont and this is all coming to an end. Arqiva Chalfont studios now closed and everyone assumes they will all be made redundant. Except me.

After starting at SSVC in 1983 I've been TUPE'd through a handful of companies at Chalfont, including Kingston In Media, Kingston Media Stream, TLI, Arqiva and now I'm back at SSVC.

Still in charge of Sound, I'm Sound Supervisor of British Forces News as well as working daily for Forces TV and I do a monthly location documentary called 'We Were There' featuring John Nicholl (former RAF pilot shot down over Iraq). The channel is available on Sky and Virgin.

Whilst the Arqiva studios were being dismantled, Studio Three was being converted into a gym. I was walking past 'the gym' one day and the door was open and I could see two guys installing exercise equipment, so I asked if I could take a picture of them and they said I could. I put the pictures on Facebook saying 'Studio Three is now a gym!'… well, the response was overwhelming, the people who had been made redundant commented, some in a rather vulgar way.

The next day my mobile rang and it was Site Security warning me that I had breached the rules and I could be marched off site. Well after a lot of grovelling, crawling and much persuasion I was let off with a warning.

Then I walked over to reception to tell receptionist Kim the funny news and at that point I noticed outside a Thames Valley Police forensics van, well, it had to be done.
I posed in front of the van and Kim the receptionist took the pic…then in spite of my telling off, I immediately posted it on Facebook saying "It wasn't my fault!"

I then received yet another 'roasting' from site services. Apparently, the night before there had been a break-in and thousands of pounds worth of equipment was stolen.

I'm going to live a quiet life now.

Forces TV is really growing now with known presenters. One of those is lovely Polly Middlehurst who works at Sky News.

In fact, I remember sitting on the couch at home with my wife, daughter and mum and Sky News was on the telly. Polly was presenting. I said to Mum "I know her!" I immediately pinged her message while she was reading the news.
Then the report ended and the pictures cut back to Polly who looked slightly surprised. So, I messaged her again saying "What happened there?" …seconds later she was back on tv and I heard a loud ping.

My daughter Sasha said to me "Did you send me a message dad?" I explained that I hadn't, in fact what she had heard was my message pinging on Polly's iPad on the tv!

Funny old world.

Checking out microphones on eBay in the gallery on my computer, Polly walked past me saying "You sad b*st*rd Clint looking at Sennheiser microphones!"… little pause, I said "They're not! They're Neumann!" Says it all.

Perhaps I am a sad b*st*rd.

The first time I met General Sir Mike Jackson, Head of the Army as he was then, he was in the studio learning how to deal with live interviews. We kept feeding 1kzh tone into his ear and making his voice echo back, dipping ear feeds in and out. Poor guy had no chance but he did well.

All part of the training.

I remember the second time we had him in, he was supposed to turn up around 11, so I got in at 10.30am, lighting guys and sound crews shared the same room. Picture this, I entered the lighting/sound room to witness a slumped lighting guy, legs spread out reading a large newspaper. Awkwardly, I had climb over his legs to get to the sound desk, I sat down, looked at the lighting position and lo and behold, it was Mike Jackson again, this time seeing me in trouble!

Thanks to all the celebs and production crews I've worked with for the last thirty odd years and not only making me appreciate all the aspects of sound but being a really good bunch of guys to work with.

Also an extreme thank you to **Martin Turner, Andy Rodger** and **Mark Papp** for all their help with this book.

Thanks again

Clint Nurse

Product details

Format: Kindle Edition

File Size: 216 KB

Print Length: 110 pages

Simultaneous Device Usage: Unlimited

Publisher: Clinton Nurse; 1 edition (25 Feb 2013)

Sold by: Amazon Media EU S.à r.l.

Language: English

ASIN: B00BLSRI5A